Alexander Pitzer

Ecce Deus-Homo

The work and kingdom of the Christ of Scripture

Alexander Pitzer

Ecce Deus-Homo
The work and kingdom of the Christ of Scripture

ISBN/EAN: 9783337148041

Printed in Europe, USA, Canada, Australia, Japan

Cover: Foto ©Lupo / pixelio.de

More available books at **www.hansebooks.com**

ECCE DEUS-HOMO

OR

THE WORK AND KINGDOM

OF

THE CHRIST OF SCRIPTURE.

They have taken away my Lord, and I know not where they have laid Him
MARY.

PHILADELPHIA
J. B. LIPPINCOTT & CO
1868.

Entered according to Act of Congress, in the year 1867, by
J. B. LIPPINCOTT & CO.,
In the Clerk's Office of the District Court of the United States for the Eastern District of Pennsylvania.

LIPPINCOTT'S PRESS,
Philadelphia.

CONTENTS.

CHAPTER I.
PARENTAGE AND BIRTH OF JESUS 9

CHAPTER II.
MISSION AND BAPTISM OF JOHN 25

CHAPTER III.
MISSION AND MEDIATION OF THE GOD-MAN 35

CHAPTER IV.
JESUS CHRIST AS TEACHER OF MEN 49

CHAPTER V.
THE DEATH OF CHRIST 66

CHAPTER VI.
THE RESURRECTION OF JESUS 83

CHAPTER VII.

The King and His kingdom.................. 105

CHAPTER VIII.

The Structure of Christ's kingdom............ 115

CHAPTER IX.

The Spirituality of the kingdom............... 132

CHAPTER X.

The Unity of the Church...................... 144

CHAPTER XI.

Baptism, the Law of Membership............... 164

CHAPTER XII.

The Lord's Supper, and the Law of Life....... 178

CHAPTER XIII.

The Second Coming of the Son of man........ 192

PREFACE.

THE basis upon which this work rests is that Jesus Christ was the God-man—not the Homo, merely, nor the Deus, merely, but, in His one Person, the Deus-Homo.

Upon any other theory than this, His Life, Work and Kingdom are perfectly inexplicable.

Some recent surveys of Christ and His work, that have had large circulation among thinking men, rest upon no historic foundation, because not derived from the only trustworthy documents we have concerning the Divine Man; they are dogmatic and imaginative.

I write this book because I love Him who loved me, and gave Himself for me; and I wish to make known to others the loveliness of Jesus; and to Him, with earnest prayer to the Giver of all Good for his blessing upon my work, I now dedicate this attempt to set forth his claims and character as the Divine Man.

THE AUTHOR.

ECCE DEUS-HOMO.

CHAPTER I.

The Parentage and Birth of Jesus.

MATTHEW begins his gospel by giving us a genealogy of Jesus Christ, tracing back his descent, through royal ancestors, to Abraham, the father of the Hebrew people.

Luke, who has also written a biography of the God-man, traces back his descent still further, through Shem and Enoch to Adam, the father of the human race.

The first genealogy was written for the Hebrews, and the object of the writer is to show that Jesus Christ was a descendant of Abraham, with whom the covenant of circumcision, organizing the visible Church, was made. The second was written for the Gentiles, and the object of the writer is to show that Jesus was descended from the first human pair, and as such was the Saviour of the world.

Both of these biographers are very careful to state that Mary, a Jewess, was his mother, but that Joseph, her husband, was not his real, but only his reputed, father. Jesus Christ was begotten, not after a natural, but a supernatural, manner; He had no human father. When Joseph and Mary, the mother of Christ, were espoused, before they came together, it was found that Mary was great with child by the Holy Ghost, the Third Person of the Godhead. This supernatural event was not entirely unexpected to Mary. Several months before, the angel Gabriel had been sent from God to inform her that she was to conceive and bring forth a son, whose name was to be called Jesus, a Saviour, because He was to save His people from their sins. The angel also told her that this son of her's was to be the Son of the Highest, and that He was to have the throne of His great ancestor, David, for ever and ever.

Nor had Mary been left in ignorance as to the manner of her conception. The Holy Ghost was to come upon her, and the power of the Highest was to overshadow her, and the holy thing thus supernaturally begotten of her was to be called, after his birth, the Son of God.

To the people of those days, these things did not seem so remarkable: one of their old prophets, more than seven hundred years before, had declared that a virgin should conceive and bare a son, and that his name should be Immanuel, which means, God with us. The entire history, too, of this Jewish people abounded with angelic appearances, supernatural events, and Divine interpositions; their God was a very present God, a Personal Jehovah.

Mary, who was a Jewess, believed the angelic annunciation, and pondered deeply in her heart his words. There were several other supernatural events directly connected with the birth of Jesus Christ which deserve notice.

Mary had a cousin named Elizabeth, the wife of Zacharias, living in the hill country of Judea, to whose house Mary went immediately after the announcement of the Angel Gabriel; and when she entered the house of her kinswoman, who was already six months advanced in pregnancy, the babe in Elizabeth's womb leaped, and the Holy Ghost moved her to greet her kinswoman Mary thus: "Blessed art thou among women, and blessed is the fruit of thy womb. And whence is this to me, that the mother of my Lord should come to me? For, lo, as soon as the salutation of thy voice sounded in mine ears, the babe leaped in my womb for joy. And blessed is she that believed; for there shall be a performance of those things which were told her from the Lord."

Mary recognized a Divine Hand in all these wonderful events, and she saw in them the fulfillment of the gracious promises made in time past to the fathers, and her feeling found expression in the following beautiful language:

My soul doth magnify the Lord,
And my spirit hath rejoiced in God my Saviour.
For He hath regarded the low estate of His handmaiden;
For, behold, from henceforth all generations shall call me blessed.
For He that is mighty hath done to me great things;
And holy is His name.
And His mercy is on them that fear Him
From generation to generation.
He hath showed strength with His arm;
He hath scattered the proud in the imaginations of their hearts.
He hath put down the mighty from their seats,
And exalted them of low degree.
He hath filled the hungry with good things;
And the rich hath He sent away empty.
He hath holpen His servant Israel,
In remembrance of His mercy;
As He spake to our fathers,

To Abraham, and to his seed for ever.

Mary abode with Elizabeth three months, and then returned to her own home in Nazareth of Galilee, where her espoused husband Joseph also lived. After her return, Joseph became aware of her condition, and was minded to put her away privily; but an angel appeared unto him in a dream, and warned him against so doing, saying, Joseph, thou son of David, fear not to take unto thee Mary thy wife, for that which is conceived in her is of the Holy Ghost; and she shall bring forth a son, and thou shalt call his name Jesus; for He shall save His people from their sins. Being thus warned, Joseph took her as his wife, but knew her not until she had brought forth her first-born.

Soon after Joseph had been warned, and before Jesus was born, a decree went out from Cæsar Augustus, the emperor of the vast Roman empire of which Judea was a conquered province, that an assessment of all the inhabitants of his empire should be made for the purpose of levying a tax. The tax was not collected until several years after the enrollment, when Cyrenius was governor of Syria.

In accordance with this decree of Cæsar Augustus, Joseph went up from the city of Nazareth in Galilee, with Mary his wife, now great with child, to Bethlehem of Judea, the city of David, because he was of the house and lineage of David, to be assessed for his tax.

While they were in Bethlehem the days were accomplished that Mary should be delivered, and she brought forth her first-born son, and wrapped him in swaddling-clothes, and laid him in a manger, because there was no room for them in the inn. The birth of the Divine human male child was not unattended with miraculous events.

In the country near Bethlehem there were certain shepherds abiding in the field, keeping watch over their flocks by night. And lo, the angel of the Lord came upon them, and the glory of the Lord shone round about them; and they were sore afraid. But the angel said unto them, Fear not: for behold, I bring you good tidings of great joy, which shall be to all people. For unto you is born this day, in the city of David, a Saviour, which is Christ the Lord. And then the angel tells them how they are to recognize this Saviour Christ, in whom all people are to be blessed. They were to find the babe wrapped in swaddling-clothes, lying in the manger in Bethlehem. Scarcely had the angel given the shepherds the sign, when suddenly there was with the angel a multitude of the heavenly host, praising God, and saying,

Glory to God in the highest, and on earth peace, good-will toward man. Having chanted the Gloria in Excelsis, the angelic host returned to their home in heaven. And the shepherds, recovering from their surprise, said one to another, Let us now go even unto Bethlehem, and see this thing which is come to pass, which the Lord hath made known unto us. And they came with haste, and found Mary and Joseph, and the babe lying in the manger, even as the angel had said. Having made known publicly what they had heard and seen, the shepherds returned to their flocks.

Jesus was a Jewish child and born under the ancient covenant of circumcision; and in accordance with the law of that covenant he was circumcised upon the eighth day, and received the name Jesus, as the angel had commanded.

When the days of her purification were ended, Mary and Joseph brought Jesus to Jerusalem to present him to the Lord, and to make the offering required by the Mosaic law. While they were in Jerusalem, the Holy Ghost revealed unto a just and devout man named Simeon, who waited for the consolation of Israel, that he should not see death until he had seen the Lord's Christ; and he came by the Spirit into the temple, and he took up Jesus in his arms, and blessed God and said,

Lord, now lettest thou Thy servant depart in peace, according to Thy word:

For mine eyes have seen Thy salvation, which thou hast prepared before the face of all people;

A Light to lighten the Gentiles,

And the glory of Thy people Israel.

And Simeon blessed Joseph and Mary, and said to Mary, Behold, this child is set for the fall and rising again of many in Israel; and for a sign which shall be spoken against.

Not long after this, certain magi, or wise men from the East, came to Jerusalem, saying, Where is He that is born King of the Jews, for we have seen his star in the East, and have come to worship Him. Hearing this remarkable statement, King Herod gathered the chief priests and scribes, and demanded of them where Christ should be born; and they, referring to the old prophetic books of the Jews, said: In Bethlehem of Judea, for thus it is written in the prophet Micah. King Herod then sent the wise men to Bethlehem to find the royal child, and commanded them, if they found Him, to bring him word, so that he also might go and worship Him; his real motive was, however, that he might kill the child, and thus save himself from a rival in Him who was born King of the Jews. As the wise men departed, lo, the star they had seen in the East went before them until it came and stood over where the young child was. And when they were come into the house, they saw the young child with Mary His mother, and they fell down and worshiped Him; and when they had opened their treasures, they presented unto Him gifts—gold, and frankincense, and myrrh. And being warned of God not to return unto Herod, they departed into their own country another way.

The advent of this Supernatural Being into our world is attended with miraculous events, angelic appearances, and Divine interpositions. To him who believes in a Personal God, a created universe, and the trustworthiness of human testimony, all these statements concerning the parentage and birth of Jesus Christ are clear, consistent, and credible. These biographies record the birth of a Supernatural Being; the Incarnation of the Son of God; the formation of a human body and soul in the womb of a virgin by the direct agency of the Holy Ghost; and the eternal union of this manhood, thus supernaturally generated, with the Second Person of the Godhead. And this Holy Thing is at once the Son of God and the Son of Mary —the Son of the Highest and the Son of Man. He is indeed the Deus-Homo, the God-man; He is Jesus and He is Christ, and, as such, the Saviour of the world.

To him who denies the personality of the Deity and the fact of a creation, and the trustworthiness of these biographies as historic documents, of course all these statements made by the writers of the Gospel history are impossible and incredible, and the whole story is a legend or myth, or both. For miracles are impossible unless there be a Personal God and a created universe. It is said that these facts are miraculous, and that hence they are incredible, because they contradict all human experience. But if the most ancient records of the race be reliable, if any human testimony or historic documents be trustworthy, then the facts narrated by the four Evangelists do not contradict all human experience. It is true that the men of this generation have not been eye-witnesses of miracles, but the men of this generation are but a part of the whole race. And the ancient histories of the Jews—the oldest and most reliable of all histories—are filled with records of angelic appearances, supernatural events, and Divine interpositions; and if these historic documents are rejected because they contain records of miracles, then the whole science of historical criticism is at an end, and no fact of a past age can be substantiated by any amount of testimony. And if there be a Personal God, surely He can operate whenever and however

He may please upon a universe that He has created.

And even grant that no miracle had ever been wrought before the incarnation of the Son of God; is the *negative* testimony of all the men who lived before that day to invalidate the *positive* testimony of scores and hundreds of competent and credible witnesses of that day, who testify, in the most solemn manner, that they saw miracles wrought? If all the generations who lived before the Incarnation had been present in Judea when these miraculous events are reported to have occurred, and if they had affirmed, from actual observation, knowledge and experience, that the events did not occur, then we might lay stress upon the argument from universal experience; but, as they were not there, their testimony is perfectly valueless.

Are the steam engine and the magnetic telegraph to be accounted myths or legends because the universal experience of man up to the days of Watt and Morse had never witnessed any such things? Could not millions of men, if they had power to speak from their graves, testify that no steam engine or magnetic telegraph had ever drawn a train or carried a message since the creation of the world? Do not these inventions contradict all human experience, and are they not therefore impossible and incredible? Will the advocates of the "experience" argument risk that argument by laying their necks upon the iron rail as the express train thunders along the track? They have all human experience for more than five thousand years to prove that their necks are safe. Either one of two things—we must accept as true these supernatural events connected with the birth of Jesus Christ, or else we must reject the whole science of historic criticism and the whole law of human testimony: there is no middle ground. It is sad to see the dogmatism and crude fancies and impossible conjectures of modern rationalists, when they refuse to accept the supernatural facts of Gospel history. In their anxiety to get rid of the Divine and superhuman element of the Gospel, they are driven into conjectures and hypotheses more improbable than the miracles which they deny.

Matthew and Luke, looking earthward, write of Jesus as the Son of Mary—the Human, the Homo. Mark, in his biography, declares that Jesus Christ was the Son of God. The gentle and loving John, gazing into heaven itself, sees the Eternal Son upon His Father's throne, and thus begins in solemn strain his lofty theme: In the beginning was the Word, and the Word was with God, and the Word was God. Jesus

Christ, then, is both Human and Divine—God and Man; He is the Deus-Homo.

The proofs of His humanity are abundant and conclusive; but it was a sinless, supernatural humanity. So also the proofs of His Divinity are abundant and conclusive; but it was not Divinity afar off, but nigh to man—nay, man's elder brother. He had an earthly human mother; His human body and soul were formed in her womb and of her substance; He was born, He ate, He slept, He drank, He grew— He lived, He loved, He sorrowed, He died. Herein, He was of the earth, earthy; of humanity, human. But He says, Before Abraham was, I am. He was the only Son, eternally begotten of the Father; the brightness of His glory, and the express image of His person. Nay, He and the Father are one; He possessed power over creation which belonged only to Deity; He opened the eyes of the blind, unstopped the ears of the deaf, cleansed the lepers, multiplied the loaves, calmed the tempest, healed the sick and raised the dead; herein He was Divine—manifestly He must be called Immanuel, God with us, the Wonderful, the Counsellor, the Father of Eternity, the Prince of Peace, the Deus-Homo, the God-man Christ Jesus.

It is of the utmost importance to bear in mind

these fundamental facts of the Incarnation, for upon these depend absolutely the life and work of the God-man; for if He be not Divine and human, then the record of His life and death is the most inexplicable of all human writings, and we are left without any key to unlock the mysteries of Gospel history. But with the facts of His Incarnation in our hands, we may walk safely amid all the grand mysteries of Godliness, great as they are: God manifest in the flesh, justified in the Spirit, seen of angels, preached unto the Gentiles, believed on in the world, received up into glory.

The four biographers have preserved but one incident in the life of Jesus from His childhood to His public ministry. His parents went up to Jerusalem every year to the great Jewish feast of the Passover. When Jesus was twelve years old they carried him with them. When the feast was ended, Joseph and Mary returned, but Jesus tarried behind in Jerusalem. His parents, supposing that he was in the returning company, went a day's journey from the city and sought the child among their kinsfolk; and not finding him, they returned to Jerusalem seeking for him. They found him in the temple, seated in the midst of the doctors, both hearing them and asking them questions. And all who heard him were astonished at his understanding and answers. His mother was amazed, and said, Son, why hast Thou dealt thus with us? Thy father and I have sought Thee sorrowing. He said unto them, How is that ye sought me? wist ye not that I must be about my Father's business. This surely is a very undutiful reply from the child if He be the mere boy Jesus. But if He be the eternal Son of the Heavenly Father, as well as the Son of the Virgin Mother, then surely it became Him thus to do and thus to speak, for He was His mother's Lord no less than her son.

"I must be about my Father's business." This expression of the youthful Christ gives us the clue to His whole subsequent life. This is the one grand idea ever before His mind. As the Divine boy in the temple, it is His Father's business that engages Him; as the Great Teacher of mankind, it is His Father's will that He makes known; as the Mediator between God and man, He does not His own will, but the will of Him who sent Him; as both Priest and Victim, in the anguish of the garden and the agony of the cross, He still pleads that His Father's will may be done; and though a Son, and at once Divine and human, yet still learned He obedience by the things which He suffered. This Christ of God is not some wondrous man waking up to the consciousness that he possesses superhuman power; He is not some high creature of God coming from heavenly lands to teach men how to live, and showing them how to die; but He is the Only Begotten of His Father, the eternal Son coming down from the skies, to be made flesh and dwell among us, that He may ever be about His Father's business, and finish the work His Father gave Him to do.

The grand objective point in the life of the God-man was not the mount from which He delivered his immortal sermon; nor the beautiful waters of Tiberias over which He sailed, and whose tempest He calmed; nor the Garden of Gethsemane where He sweat great drops of blood; nor Bethany, where He raised the dead; nor Calvary, where He himself tasted death; nor the Mount of Olives from which He ascended. His Omniscient eye swept far away beyond these; beyond the mount, beyond the sea, beyond the garden, beyond the cross, away off into the eternal world, there where the joy was set before Him—that joy which enabled Him to endure the cross and despise the shame—to do His Father's will and His Father's work, and then to make known His Father's glory to the principalities and powers in heavenly places throughout the everlasting ages—this was the grand object ever before Him, and most sublimely did He accomplished the aim and end of His life.

CHAPTER II.

Mission and Baptism of John.

THE people of Judea were eagerly expecting the advent of a superhuman being. Their old prophetical books, which were held in the highest esteem by all the people, had spoken in stirring strains of a Messiah who was to come. These books spoke of Him as a Prophet, like unto Moses, but wiser than Moses; as the Son of David, who was to sit upon David's throne for ever; as the Priest higher than Aaron, who was head of the whole sacerdotal order. To prepare the minds of His countrymen for the advent of Messiah, a forerunner had appeared in the person of John the Baptist.

As has been already stated, John was a kinsman of Jesus, for his mother Elizabeth was cousin to Mary, the mother of Jesus, and it was to the house of Elizabeth that Mary went when she knew that she was with child by the Holy Ghost, and the unborn babe in Elizabeth's womb leaped when the voice of Mary sounded in the ears of his mother.

Zacharias, the husband of Elizabeth, went into the temple to burn incense before the Lord, and there appeared unto him the angel of the Lord standing on the right side of the altar of incense. And the angel said unto him, Fear not, Zacharias, for thy prayer is heard, and thy wife Elizabeth shall bear thee a son, and thou shalt call his name John; and thou shalt have joy and gladness, and many shall rejoice at his birth. For he shall be great in the sight of the Lord, and shall drink neither wine nor strong drink, and he shall be filled with the Holy Ghost even from his mother's womb. And many of the children of Israel shall he turn to the Lord their God; and he shall go before Him in the spirit and power of Elias to turn the hearts of the fathers to the children, and the disobedient to the wisdom of the just, to make ready a people prepared for the Lord.

In accordance with the promise of the angel, Elizabeth, who was barren and well-stricken in years, conceived and bare a son, and called his name John.

His father Zacharias, who had been dumb since the angel appeared to him in the temple, as a sign to him that what the angel said would come to pass, now received the use of speech again, and in answer to the inquiry concerning

John, What manner of child shall this be? moved by the Holy Ghost, thus spake:

And thou, child,
Shall be called the Prophet of the Highest,
For thou shalt go before the face of the Lord to prepare His ways;
To give knowledge unto His people,
By the remission of their sins,
Through the tender mercy of our God;
Whereby the Day-spring from on high hath visited us,
To give light to them that sit in darkness and in the shadow of death,
To guide our feet into the way of peace.

This son of Elizabeth and Zacharias was circumcised on the eighth day, and received the name of John. The child grew, and waxed strong in the spirit, and was in the desert until the day of his showing unto Israel.

The following points of resemblance between John the forerunner and Jesus the Messiah are to be noted, viz:

1st. They were kinsmen—their mothers were cousins.

2d. The birth of each of them had been announced by an angel.

3d. They were supernaturally conceived in the wombs of their mothers: Mary, the mother of Jesus, was a virgin; Elizabeth, the mother of John, was barren, and was, moreover, past the age of child-bearing.

4th. Very little is known of either of them from their childhood to their public ministry.

5th. They were both prophets, and proclaimed a baptism; and the Greater was baptised by the Less.

6th. They were together upon the Mount of Transfiguration.

7th. They were both executed by the civil authorities—John was beheaded by King Herod, Jesus was crucified under Pontius Pilate.

From the days of Haggai and Malachi, prophets of the restoration, until the days of John, a period of over four hundred years, no inspired prophet had appeared among the children of Israel.

When Tiberius Cæsar had been upon the Roman throne fifteen years, when Pilate was governor of Judea, when Herod was tetrarch of Galilee, and Annas and Caiaphas were high priests, the Word of God came unto John, the son of Zacharias, in the wilderness.

John was at this time about thirty years of age; his raiment was made of camel's hair, and bound round his loins with a leathern girdle; his food was locusts and wild honey. Suddenly, and without any warning, he appears before the people of Judea with the startling message,

Repent ye, for the kingdom of heaven is at hand. The stern prophet comes unannounced from the wilderness to prepare the way of the Lord.

His wild appearance, his authoritative command, his startling announcement, his pungent preaching, and the general expectation on the part of the people of the coming Messiah, all combined to give wonderful success to the ministry of the Baptist. Pharisees, Sadducees, Scribes, publicans, lawyers and soldiers flock by thousands to his preaching.

The substance of John's preaching was:

1st. He was not the Promised Messiah.

2d. He was the Messiah's forerunner, to prepare the way of the Lord.

3d. The forerunner was to decrease, but Messiah was to increase.

4th. The kingdom of heaven was at hand.

5th. Men must now repent, and be baptized for the remission of sins.

6th. The baptism which John administered was to make Messiah manifest to Israel; and the sign whereby John would know the Messiah was the descent of the Holy Ghost.

7th. When Messiah was manifested, he would baptize with the Holy Ghost and fire.

One day, as John was preaching and baptizing at the river Jordan, Jesus Christ, now about thirty years of age, went out to the Wilderness Prophet to receive baptism at his hands.

John appears to have had some presentiment that Jesus was the Messiah, and attempted to dissuade him, saying, I have need to be baptized of Thee, and comest Thou to me? But Jesus insisted that thus it became him to fulfill all righteousness, and then John administered to him the ordinance of baptism. After the baptism, the Spirit of God, in the form of a dove, descended and lighted upon the head of Jesus; and an audible voice came from the Father in heaven, saying, This is my beloved Son, in whom I am well pleased. After this Divine manifestation and declaration, John knew that Jesus Christ was the promised Messiah, and he bare record that this was the Son of God, and cried, Behold the Lamb of God (Ecce agnus Dei), that taketh away the sin of the world. Thus at the baptism, as at the birth of the God-man, there are Divine interpositions, heavenly announcements, and supernatural events.

After Jesus had entered upon His public ministry, He said unto the multitudes concerning John, What went ye out into the wilderness to see? John the Baptist was not a reed shaken by the wind; he was not a man of changeable, uncertain, and fickle purpose and judgment, carried about with every wind of doctrine—shaken in his views as the reed is shaken by the wind.

Nor was he a man to wear soft raiment and live in kings' houses; he was not a man to fawn upon those in authority, and turn and shape his views to meet the wishes and desires of those who had authority among their fellow-men.

But he was a Prophet, and more than a Prophet; he was indeed My messenger, called of God, to go before Me, in the spirit and power of Elijah, to prepare the way of the Lord.

Among them that are born of woman—that is, of all those born under the ancient covenant, that covenant made in the flesh, and after the flesh, after the law of natural birth—there has not risen a greater than John the Baptist; notwithstanding, he that is least in the kingdom of heaven—that is, least enlightened under this new and better covenant, this dispensation of My personal ministry and the descent of the Holy Ghost—is greater than he. John came in a *transition* period, and was the transition prophet. The Old Dispensation was passing away, and the New Dispensation was coming in, and his ministry was partly in the Old and partly in the New Dispensation. He was greater than any prophet before him under the Old Dispensation, for he saw the Messiah and the descent of the Spirit; he was less than any prophet under the New Dispensation, for he did not see the Holy Ghost *poured out* upon the day of Pentecost, and the Christian Church fully inaugurated.

Jesus asked the people this question: The baptism of John, whence was it? from heaven or of man?

Undoubtedly, it was from heaven, but it was not Christian baptism.

John was a prophet under the covenant of circumcision; he was raised up, called and qualified by God as a preacher and baptizer under that covenant. He was commissioned by Jehovah to declare His will and to administer the baptism of repentance—but all of John's work was wholly *preparatory;* he was the forerunner of Messiah, and Messiah's kingdom; and his baptism was *preparatory* to Christian baptism. Jesus, as born under the covenant of circumcision, and as a minister of that covenant, received the baptism that John administered; but, though the baptism of John was from heaven, it was not Christian baptism, as is evident—

1st. It was a baptism administered while the old covenant of circumcision was in full force, and before the dispensation of ceremonies had passed away. The veil of the temple was not yet rent in token that the ancient economy was fulfilled.

2d. John's baptism was before Jesus was manifested as the Messiah; and one special purpose to be served by that baptism was to make Jesus known as the Messiah Saviour.

3d. It was a baptism of a kingdom of heaven *at hand*, not of a kingdom of heaven fully come and set up.

4th. It was a baptism of mere repentance, not a baptism of regeneration.

5th. It was a baptism of mere water, not of the Holy Ghost, for the Spirit was not yet given; and it was the especial perogative of the Messiah to baptize with the Holy Ghost.

6th. It was not administered in the name of the Holy Trinity—the Father, Son, and Holy Ghost.

7th. After the institution of Christian baptism by Messiah, and the descent of the Holy Ghost, the disciples of John, who had received his baptism, were *re-baptized* in token of its insufficiency.

Briefly, then, John's baptism was preparatory—of water merely, unto mere repentance, before the Mosaic Ritual was fulfilled and abrogated, before the Christian dispensation was established, and before the Messiah had a single disciple. It did not typify or symbolize the Spirit, and it was not in the name of the Trinity—Father, Son, and Spirit.

John, having prepared the way for the promised Messiah, having appeared in the spirit and power of Elias, having turned the hearts of the fathers to the children, having baptized and thus made manifest the Messiah, begins to decrease, and Messiah begins to increase; He commenced His ministry in Galilee by proclaiming the gospel of the kingdom of God.

CHAPTER III.

The Mission and Mediation of the God-man.

IF any being in the universe is competent to give us true information concerning the mission of the God-man, it is Jesus Christ himself. And whatever may be unsatisfactory in the present or past conceptions of apostles or priests, or prophets or preachers concerning His mission, surely we may rely upon the statements of Jesus as true, for He declared that He was not only the Way and the Life, but that He was the Truth.

He summed it up in a few brief sentences: I am come to seek and to save the lost, and to glorify My Father in heaven, by finishing the work He gave Me to do. It is rest and peace on earth for weary man, and it is glory to God for evermore in the highest—it is to save sinful man and to glorify his Father, God. It was not to mature plans for universal empire; not to work miracles; not to expound the true code of morals; not to display the method of the Divine government; not to reform men; not to remove evils; not to propound political dogmas; not to leave a perfect example; not to die the martyrs' death, but to save man from sin and hell, and to glorify God throughout the eternal ages.

In accomplishing these ends, it is true that He will work miracles, He will teach all moral truth, He will display the method of God's government, He will reform men, He will remove evils, He will leave a perfect example, He will die the death of the cross; but all these are incidental and ancillary—He does these things in order to the others. He teaches, He works miracles, He lives, He dies, that man may be saved from sin and hell, and that His Father may be glorified. And this two-fold work of saving man, and displaying His Father's glories to the whole intelligent creation, absolutely demands that He shall be at once both human and Divine; that He shall be the God-man Mediator Christ Jesus. He cannot save man, unless He has man's nature; He cannot perfectly and infinitely display and declare the Divine character, unless He has God's nature; He must be one with man, whom He saves, and one with God, whom He glorifies.

In the mysterious Incarnation of the Son of God, and the miraculous constitution of the person of the God-man, the following facts are abundantly evident from the writings of the evangelists and apostles:

The Divine and human natures, indissolubly united in the person of the Son of God, preserved each the properties peculiar to its own nature. No change was made in the Divine nature; there was a partial obscuration of the Divine Glory, but the nature remained the same; Deity was not changed into humanity. Nor was any change made in the human nature; it had no separate personality—the intellect and will of the man Jesus had its subsistence in the person of the Son of God; humanity was not changed into Deity.

The two natures were united in one person; they were not mixed or blended.

Whatever was predicable of either nature was predicable of the God-man, Christ Jesus.

God could not die, yet the God-man Christ Jesus did die.

Man could not create, yet the God-man Christ Jesus did create.

The humanity of Jesus had no existence before the Incarnation; yet Christ could say, Before Abraham was, I am.

The Divinity of Christ had no body, parts, or passions; yet the Church was purchased with His own blood.

Jesus Christ possessed the essential properties

of both natures, but they were not divided or separable, nor changed, nor confused, nor mixed; they were indissolubly united in one person.

Beyond doubt there are mysteries here—mysteries higher than the heights, deeper than the depths; mysteries of the Eternal, the Infinite, the Unfathomable; mysteries of uncreated existence made flesh; mysteries of God fashioned as man, dwelling among men. What is man that he shall refuse to believe the words of the Most High because he cannot comprehend the rationale of the Divine existence, the precise method and manner of the Incarnation? We are here dealing with facts, not with philosophy; and shall we reject facts, established by competent and credible witnesses, because we cannot fully comprehend the nature of the facts established? God does not call upon us to comprehend the philosophy of the Incarnation; He commands us to believe the facts of the Incarnation, and to trust in His Incarnate Son. The cry of the heathen governor, the pagan Pilate, was, Ecce Homo—Behold the Man. The command of God, and the cry of the Scripture is, Ecce Deus-Homo—Behold the God-man. No wonder that they who come to see the mere man are amazed and confounded; it is not a man, but a Divine man, of whom these biographers write. They narrate the life of the Super-human. These records tell of God coming down from heaven to operate upon a universe that He created; they tell of angels and miracles and Divine handiwork. Is there no existence above matter? Is there no cause except antecedence and sequence? Is there no life higher than that of nature? Is there no truth in the universal consciousness of the race that answers back to these grand mysteries of the Supernatural, the Divine? Is there no substance casting these shadows so dark and deep across the soul? Why does the heart of man ever answer back, in cries almost divine, to the infinite heights and depths of God's revelation to a lost and guilty race? We can believe the *facts* of revelation; we cannot find out the Almighty unto perfection.

But the Son of Man came to seek and to save the lost; the God-man was a Mediator between God and men; God was in Christ reconciling the world unto Himself, not imputing their trespasses unto them. Jesus Christ was a Reconciler, a Daysman, a Mediator; and as there is one God and one race, so there is but one Mediator between God and men—the man Christ Jesus.

Mediation implies estrangement and alienation; reconciliation implies enmity and hatred.

The whole need not a physician, but they who are sick. Friends have no need of mediators and reconcilers. Is it true that there is alienation and estrangement between God and man? is a Mediator and Reconciler needed between them? Surely, something has gone wrong with our world and with the race; man has departed from God; the younger son has gone into a strange country; one sheep of the hundred has gone astray; one of the pieces of money is lost. The carnal mind is enmity against God, not subject to His law, neither indeed can be; and that enmity is strong and deep and bitter. Man hates God with an intense hatred, and had he the power he would hurl Him from His throne.

God, on His part, is angry with the wicked every day; and the wrath of God is revealed from heaven against all ungodliness and unrighteousness of man.

Jesus Christ Himself ever speaks of man as a sinner, at enmity with God; and says, I am not come to call the righteous, but sinners to repentance. Come unto Me, all ye that labor and are heavy laden, and I will give you rest. It is a faithful saying, and worthy of all acceptation, that Christ Jesus came into the world to save sinners.

Man is guilty; man is depraved; man is

miserable. Guilt is wrong-doing and liability to punishment; depravity is corruption of the moral nature; misery is the suffering consequent upon guilt and depravity;

> "There is no God, the foolish saith;
> But none, There is no sorrow;"

and the universality of sorrow proves the universality of sin.

Where there is no law, there cannot be guilt or depravity or misery; for where there is no law, there is no transgression, and hence no liability to punishment; where there is no law, there is no depravity, for depravity is the want of the rectitude demanded by the law; where there is no law, there is no suffering, for suffering is the penalty of violated law. If there be no penalty, there is no law; for law without a sanction or penalty is no longer law, but mere advice.

But law is the all-pervading principle of the universe; in its silent but resistless operations it controls every particle of this boundless creation—law in the world of matter, law in the world of Providence, law in the world of spirit. We may not see the Hand that drives the machinery of the universe; we do see that it moves, and that it always moves in accordance with law. Law governs the fall of the apple to the earth, the course of the sun in his circuit. In accordance with law, men live and die; in accordance with law, nations flourish and decay. Everything that lives and moves and dies, lives, moves and dies under the operation of law.

Man cannot escape from law, or the Infinite Lawgiver; if he ascend up to heaven, law is there in all its beauty and all its glory; if he descend to hell, law is there in all its strength and all its vengeance; if he take the wings of the morning and dwell in the uttermost parts of the earth, even there shall the law claim him as its subject, and the Lawgiver hold him in His power. Law may be violated, but violation is not its abrogation. Man sinning, is still subject—still bound to obey, and bound to endure the penalty.

For six thousand long and weary years the wail of a lost creation, groaning and travailing in pain because of a broken law, has gone up to the ears of the Lord of hosts. The order of creation has been disarranged; the harmony of the universe has been broken; the world is not what it once was: some discordant element has gotten into the machinery; the great wheels still go on in their revolutions—law remains the same—but the wheels now go grinding and groaning as if in pain, by reason of the introduction of sin. The whole creation travaileth in anguish, waiting the hour of its redemption. Fierce tornadoes and horrid simoons sweep over the globe; volcanoes belch forth fire and brimstone, and whole regions of the earth and mighty cities are buried in ashes and lava; the earth opens her yawning jaws and devours her guilty inhabitants; scorpions, serpents, vermin and reptiles infest the homes of the children of men; deadly miasmas exhale from green-mantled pools, breeding disease and death; the pestilence walks in darkness and the destruction wastes at noonday; criminal laws provide penalties for wrong-doing, and jails and penitentiaries and gallows inflict punishment upon transgressors; cruel and bloody wars decimate the nations of the earth; theft and adultery and murder stalk through the land; altars, among all people, and in all countries, reek with the blood of victims, slain to appease the wrath of angered deities; surely the curse of a broken law rests upon man and upon the earth.

When we pursue the investigation, and look into the depths of man's moral nature, there too we find marks of disorder, ruin, and sin. The mind is darkened; the desires are corrupt; the affections depraved; the will is capricious; the emotions are perverse; and conscience thunders wrathfully from his throne in the human breast. Man's deepest conviction is that he is guilty, and his heart yearns for a better land.

Meantime the Holy God sits upon His throne of justice, proclaiming His infinite hatred of sin, and revealing His wrath against all the workers of iniquity; and the law, never abating one jot or tittle of its demands, declares that the sinner shall die.

In such a posture of affairs, and between these two parties, Jesus of Nazareth appears as a Daysman, a Mediator, a Peace-maker, a Reconciler. In the midst of earth's darkness, He comes to give light; in the midst of earth's sorrow, He comes to give peace; in the midst of earth's death, He comes to give life.

In order to be a mediator, certain qualifications are requisite on the part of him who undertakes this office; and the higher the character of the parties to be reconciled, the more exalted must be the qualifications of him who attempts the work of mediation. God is one of these parties, and He is Infinite; man is the other, and he is Finite. Now mark how the very constitution of His person fits Him for His office as Mediator. As the Only Begotten of the Father, the Son of the Highest, Deity Incarnate, God manifest in the flesh, He is most intimately connected with God; nay, He is One with God, nay He is God, and therefore Infinite, and possessed of infinite qualifications; as the Son of the Virgin, the Seed of the Woman, the Second

Adam, He is our elder brother, and Finite—and so the Infinite-Finite Mediator.

If He be not Infinite, He cannot satisfy the demands of a broken infinite law; finite obedience or finite suffering must be eternal in order to meet the demands of an Infinite law.

Again, the Mediator must be Divine in order to send the Comforter, the Holy Ghost, to recreate, in the image of God, the moral nature of man.

And He must have Infinite power, in order that He may conquer all of our enemies, and overcome death, hell and the grave.

But if the Mediator be merely Divine, then He is infinitely removed from man—His mediation is too exalted to be efficacious; and as He laid hold of the seed of Abraham to save man, He must be made like unto His brethren. As the children who are to be redeemed are partakers of flesh and blood, the Redeemer must likewise be partaker of the same, that so He may be a merciful and faithful High Priest, having a fellow feeling with our infirmities.

As God and as Man, as God-man Mediator, He stands between the Infinite and the Finite; between His Father God in heaven, and His brother man on earth; and now God in Christ is reconciling the world unto Himself, not imputing their trespasses unto them.

Meantime the Holy God sits upon His throne of justice, proclaiming His infinite hatred of sin, and revealing His wrath against all the workers of iniquity; and the law, never abating one jot or tittle of its demands, declares that the sinner shall die.

In such a posture of affairs, and between these two parties, Jesus of Nazareth appears as a Daysman, a Mediator, a Peace-maker, a Reconciler. In the midst of earth's darkness, He comes to give light; in the midst of earth's sorrow, He comes to give peace; in the midst of earth's death, He comes to give life.

In order to be a mediator, certain qualifications are requisite on the part of him who undertakes this office; and the higher the character of the parties to be reconciled, the more exalted must be the qualifications of him who attempts the work of mediation. God is one of these parties, and He is Infinite; man is the other, and he is Finite. Now mark how the very constitution of His person fits Him for His office as Mediator. As the Only Begotten of the Father, the Son of the Highest, Deity Incarnate, God manifest in the flesh, He is most intimately connected with God; nay, He is One with God, nay He is God, and therefore Infinite, and possessed of infinite qualifications; as the Son of the Virgin, the Seed of the Woman, the Second

Adam, He is our elder brother, and Finite—and so the Infinite-Finite Mediator.

If He be not Infinite, He cannot satisfy the demands of a broken infinite law; finite obedience or finite suffering must be eternal in order to meet the demands of an Infinite law.

Again, the Mediator must be Divine in order to send the Comforter, the Holy Ghost, to recreate, in the image of God, the moral nature of man.

And He must have Infinite power, in order that He may conquer all of our enemies, and overcome death, hell and the grave.

But if the Mediator be merely Divine, then He is infinitely removed from man—His mediation is too exalted to be efficacious; and as He laid hold of the seed of Abraham to save man, He must be made like unto His brethren. As the children who are to be redeemed are partakers of flesh and blood, the Redeemer must likewise be partaker of the same, that so He may be a merciful and faithful High Priest, having a fellow feeling with our infirmities.

As God and as Man, as God-man Mediator, He stands between the Infinite and the Finite; between His Father God in heaven, and His brother man on earth; and now God in Christ is reconciling the world unto Himself, not imputing their trespasses unto them.

But any mediation that will prove effectual must respect every claim that God has upon man, and every obligation that man is under to God.

Man having violated the law, broken the covenant under which he was placed, God will no longer have any dealings of any sort whatever with him. So far as God is concerned the case is ended, for the sanction of the law was, do and live—disobey and die; man failed to do, and hence forfeited his life; he disobeyed, and hence he must die. All that the Infinite God can ever say to the sinner is, Thou hast broken the law, and thou must die. Hence the absolute necessity of a Mediator and Daysman between God and man.

There is a popular and prevalent idea that, somehow or in some way, Christ as Mediator modified the demands of the law; that He lessened the precept and mitigated the penalty of the law; that, in virtue of His work, something of the justice of the Divine government was held in abeyance. To believe thus is totally to misunderstand the nature of His mediation. I am not come, said Jesus Himself, to destroy the law or the prophets, but to fulfill; for until heaven and earth shall pass away, not one jot or tittle of the law shall pass away until all be fulfilled. Nay, in order that the mediation of

Jesus Christ may be made efficacious to the saving of sinners, He Himself must so obey the precept, and so endure the penalty of the law, that it is for ever magnified and made honorable. And, in fact, the mediatorial work of the God-man, so far from modifying the claims of the law, has afforded, to the whole intelligent creation, the very highest possible proof of the Infinite rectitude of the Divine government, and the majesty of the Divine law. God is just, even when He justifies the ungodly.

Whatever claim God ever had upon man was, and must have been, holy, just, and right; whatever obligation man was ever under to obey—or failing to obey, whatever obligation he was under to suffer the penalty—was holy, just, and right. God could not modify or lessen, or abrogate His claim, when in its very nature, the claim was holy, just, and right; the Mediator, in view of the character and claims of God, could not modify or lessen or abrogate man's obligation to obey, or to suffer, since that obligation was, in its own nature, holy, just, and right. There is an absolute necessity that the Mediator shall respect every claim of God and every obligation of man.

Human nature has sinned, hence human nature must suffer; and the Son of God, who comes as Mediator, must be partaker of human nature, so that in the likeness of sinful flesh, and as made flesh, not sinful, He may obey and suffer for man, who had sinned. He assumes a true body and reasonable soul, and suffers in the room and stead of man.

As the Son of man, he is sufficiently humbled to meet the wants of man; as the Eternal Son of God, He is sufficiently exalted to meet the claims of God, and to vindicate the majesty of the Divine law.

As a correct and legitimate interpretation of the historic records concerning the parentage and birth of Jesus Christ, absolutely demands the union of the Divine and human natures in his one Person; as the philosophical analysis of the records concerning His Person necessitates that Christ Jesus shall be both God and Man; so here again any true conception of His mediatorial office and work forces us to the conclusion that Jesus Christ, as Mediator between God and man, is, indeed, the Deus-Homo, the God-man.

CHAPTER IV.

Jesus Christ as Teacher of Men.

JESUS CHRIST was about thirty years of age when He began his public ministry as a Teacher sent from God. He was inducted into His office by His great forerunner, John, and was anointed with the Holy Ghost above measure.

The Jewish ruler, Nicodemus, who came to Him by night, said unto Him, Rabbi, we know that Thou art a Teacher come from God; for no man can do these miracles that Thou doest, except God be with him. Nicodemus knew that He was a Divine Teacher because He wrought Divine works. The miracles of Jesus are the proof that He was commissioned of God to teach men; and this is the precise import of a miracle—it is a credential given by God to His messengers, to authenticate their mission; it is a credential *above nature* to attest a message *above nature*.

A miracle is not a violation of the laws of nature, nor a suspension of those laws, nor an abrogation of those laws—it is a Divine Hand let down into the machinery of creation to move it at the Divine will and pleasure. If there be no Personal God, then, of course, there is no Divine Hand to be let down; if there be no creation, then, of course, there is no machinery to be moved at all.

"The public ministry of Jesus Christ embraced a period of a little over three years; it was confined to a conquered province of the Roman empire; it was limited to his own people, the Jews—a bigoted, a peculiar, a subjugated and an exclusive people; but its results are still felt over all the earth in the rolling tide of human history; what He said can never die.

They who heard his teachings were amazed that the carpenter of Nazareth should utter such imperishable truth. And they asked, From whence hath this man these things? and what wisdom is this which is given unto Him? Is not this the carpenter, the Son of Mary, and are not His brethren and sisters here with us? The difficulty to be solved was: How can this *man*, this Son of Mary, this humble carpenter, proclaim such Divine truths, with such Divine authority, and work such miracles to attest His mission? There is something here inexplicable to human *reason;* and we need not wonder that they were offended at Him. They knew Him to be a *man*, and yet here were Divine words and Divine works—can man be Divine, or can Deity be human? If they had known the Scriptures and believed the facts of the Incarnation, the difficulty would have disappeared. It is the Deus-Homo who teaches.

As, in accordance with the saying of the Forerunner, Jesus begins to *increase*, and the fame of Him spreads throughout Judea, it is evident to all that He is a Prophet raised up of God; and the question at once arises, what Prophet is this? Is it John the Baptist risen from the dead? or is Elijah come down from heaven in his chariot of fire? Or is this indeed the very Christ, the Prophet of whom Moses did write? But how could such a Prophet arise out of Nazareth, from whence no good thing could come? And as for Christ, the Prophets declared that He should arise out of Bethlehem. They had forgotten the *birth-place* of Jesus.

These inquiries only increased the interest excited by the teachings of the Great Prophet; and immense numbers of all ranks, classes, and conditions flocked to hear Him speak; and their emphatic testimony was, that no man had ever spoken as this man spoke.

When we examine the personal instructions

of this wondrous Teacher, the following facts strike us as noteworthy, viz:

1. That so little of what He said has been put upon record, and left in a permanent form for the guidance of mankind. One of His most intimate friends, and a beloved Apostle, has told us that if all the things that Jesus did should be written, he supposes the world could hardly contain all the books. And yet a very brief portion of four very brief biographies contains all that is left on record of the teachings of the Divine Man. By all odds, the greater part of these biographies is taken up with facts, incidents and events in His life.

2. The only writing that Jesus ever did was when the woman taken in the act of adultery was brought before Him for judgment; he stooped down and wrote with His finger upon the ground, and it disappeared from the earth whereon it was written centuries ago. He left it to His contemporaries to gather up His instructions and put them into written forms, and thus transmit them to men. Is it not strange that such a Teacher, endowed with such wisdom, uttering such truth, should have left to others the compilation of His doctrines?

3. Jesus Christ as a religious Teacher never identified Himself with any school of philosophy or any sect of religion. The Pharisees as the

Ritualists, the Sadducees as the Rationalists, the Essenes as the Mystics, or the Herodians as the Patriots, would have gladly hailed Him as an accession to their party; but He stands aloof from them all; He asks, he desires no adventitious support for His doctrines; He will rely simply and wholly upon the Truth which He proclaims; this shall commend itself to every man's conscience in the sight of God. All earthly teachers take advantage of their party or sect as a means and power to propagate their views and doctrines. To estimate the power of Jesus as a Teacher, let any man, in his own strength, without aid from Church or State, party or sect, undertake to establish among men any new system of truth. He will soon find that he has attempted what he cannot perform.

4. His teachings were entirely extemporaneous. There is no evidence that He ever meditated beforehand what He would say. His discourses and doctrines were delivered, as we would say, upon the spur of the moment. Many of His most instructive sermons had their origin, as men would speak, in wholly accidental circumstances. His speech to the woman of Samaria, at Jacob's well in Sychar, had its origin in His asking her to give Him a drink of water; and such an impression did His words

make upon her mind that she returned to the city declaring that this man was the Messiah. His conversation with Nicodemus, which contains, as it were, the whole essence of revealed truth, had its origin in a night visit from a Jewish ruler. So with many of His discourses; they had their origin in some unimportant circumstance, and all of them were delivered without premeditation.

5. He makes no show of human learning; never alludes to the wise men of His own or any preceding age; never appeals to authority, with this exception, that He does repeatedly quote from the books of the Old Testament Scriptures; He appeals to these as of Divine authority, and declares, most emphatically, I am not come to destroy the Law or the Prophets, but to fulfill.

6. In the whole range of His teaching there is nothing peculiar to His own age, or the country in which He was born and reared, or the people among whom He lived; and yet the age and country and people were all peculiar. Nay, so far from being peculiar to His own age and people, many of His instructions were directly opposed to the spirit of the age, the sentiments of His countrymen, and the wishes of the people.

Compare His teachings, in this regard, with those of any other philosopher or sage, and see how much all other teachers owe the spirit of the age, and how very little Christ owes. With many the age makes the *man*—in this instance, Christ made the age, and was the Instructor of *universal man.* Would the fame of Bacon be so great had he lived in this century? Would Christ be any less were he living now?

7. Another remarkable feature in all that Christ said was the simplicity with which He spoke. His language is so simple, so natural, so clear, that the wayfaring man though a fool need not err concerning His meaning. He delivers the profoundest truths cognizable by man with such perfect simplicity that children can understand them.

8. The truth taught by Jesus Christ was not intended merely for those who heard Him, nor for the men of His own age, nor for His own countrymen; but it was truth for all men, in all lands, throughout all time. Human teachers rarely look beyond the immediate horizon; they speak, generally, to their contemporaries and countrymen; Christ's view was limited by no horizon; He spake to all men, and unto the end of time. As Christ's teachings were intended for all men, so they are adapted to all men. The words of the Deus-Homo come home alike to the heart of the savage and the sage, the prince and the peasant, the philosopher and the

rustic, the Negro and the Caucasian, the wise and the foolish, the learned and the ignorant. This truth of Jesus is water for every thirsty soul. If there be a soul, no matter what its character, and there be thirst in that soul, then here is water that will quench the thirst.

9. There is no evidence that He ever expressed the least uneasiness as to the results of His doctrine. Ye shall know the truth, and the truth shall make you free—the doctrine is not Mine, but His that sent Me. When merely human teachers deliver truth, enact laws, publish books, promulgate theories or opinions, they are exceedingly anxious as to the result of their theories, books, and doctrines; nor are they less anxious as to the reception these doctrines, books and theories will meet with from the public. Christ expresses no uneasiness, either as to the result to be accomplished or the reception to be met. True, He does not expect all who hear to believe His doctrines; on the contrary, in the parable of the sower, He teaches plainly that many will not receive the truth.

10. Those who heard Him teach, noted as remarkable in His manner of instructing the people that He taught as one having authority. And this authoritative preaching was precisely wherein He differed from the Scribes of that day. There was a Divine authority in all that

Jesus said; He did not advise; He did not speculate; He did not quote human authorities; but with the profound conviction of the truth of all that He said, He uttered that truth with the authority of God. *But I say unto you*, was His emphatic assumption of authority.

11. In all of His instructions He seems to have the same knowledge of the past and future that He has of the present. He never hesitates, He never falters upon any subject of knowledge, whether God or man or angel or devil, whether past, present, or future. On every subject He speaks with absolute certainty; and after eighteen centuries of the most intense scrutiny, no man is able to show that Jesus ever made a single mistake, in the slightest particular, upon any subject of human or heavenly knowledge. Can it be said of any other teacher that he has not made mistakes upon every subject upon which he has attempted to give information?

12. His ability and success in extricating Himself from the nets in which His enemies sought to entangle Him are infinitely removed from those of any other teacher. There were three distinct parties, each one of which sought to entrap Him in His talk, and thus destroy His influence as a religious teacher. The Pharisees, the Legalists of that day, hated Him because He rebuked their hypocrisy and self-righteousness;

they brought to Him a woman taken in the very act of adultery, and said to Him, Moses commanded in the law that such should be stoned to death, but what sayest Thou? If He shall say, Let the woman die, then the people will call Him harsh and cruel; if He shall say, Let the woman go free, then He is teaching contrary to the law. His answer utterly confounds His enemies: Let him that is without sin among you cast the first stone; and they went out from the eldest to the last; turning then to the woman, He says, Go, sin no more.

The Sadducees, the religious Rationalists, hated Him because He taught the existence of angels and spirits, and the resurrection from the dead; they came to Him and said, There were seven brothers, and the first married a wife and died, and left his widow unto his brother; and the second died and left her; and the third, unto the seventh; last of all the woman died; in the resurrection therefore whose wife shall she be? In the resurrection, they neither marry nor are given in marriage—all earthly relations cease—the children of the resurrection are as the angels. Even Moses, whom you quote as authority, teaches the resurrection of the dead. The God of Abraham, of Isaac and Jacob is not a God of the dead, but of the living.

The Herodians, the "*disloyal*" of that day,

hated Him because He refused to become a partisan; they came to Him, and asked: Is it lawful to give tribute unto Cæsar or not? If He says it is lawful, then He is not true to his country; if He says it is not lawful, then He is disloyal to Cæsar. He asks them to show Him a penny. Whose image and superscription is this? He asks; they say unto Him, Cæsar's. Then render to Cæsar the things that are Cæsar's; and unto God, the things that are God's.

13. Christ Jesus never repeats Himself. Most teachers possess themselves of a few ideas, and these they are continually repeating in every conceivable form. Christ's doctrines are always new. Whenever He speaks, there comes forth from His lips some new and hitherto unknown doctrine. And it may be safely affirmed that every parable that He uttered contained a new and distinct truth; and that every discourse delivered by Him was different from every other one. Human teachers soon exhaust themselves, but Christ seems inexhaustible.

14. The form in which He uttered most of His doctrine was the parable. The Prophets had foretold that the Messiah, when He came, would teach the people in parables; so that the very *form* of the teachings of the God-man was a proof that He was the Anointed of God. I

do not know that it is possible to define a parable—it is unlike any other form of words used among men. It is not simile, or allegory, or analogy, and yet it combines some of the characteristics of all these. By using, in a figurative manner, the occupations, incidents and images of everyday life and nature, the Great Teacher conveys *spiritual* truths otherwise unknown to men. One peculiarity of the parable is, that it seizes upon some great principle that pervades the world of nature and spirit, and by the operation of the principle in nature it illustrates the operation of the principle in the world of spirit; the parables of the sower, of the tares, of the mustard-seed, of the leaven, are of this character. The parable conveys the most profound and recondite truth in so simple and natural a manner that after its exposition the wonder with every man is, that he did not sooner see the truth conveyed.

15. The subject-matter of the Messiah's teachings is no less remarkable than the manner thereof. Being the Eternal Son of God, He came forth from the bosom of the Father to make known to men the nature and attributes of the Godhead. Christ was a Revealer of God —of the mode of the Divine existence, of His character, of His works, of His ways, of His

government, of His will. The hitherto "Unknown God," whom the nations of the earth ignorantly worshiped, was now made known to men by Him who was the Brightness of His Glory, the Express Image of His Person. And it is not too much to assert that the race has obtained more true knowledge of God from the teachings of the God-man than from all other sources combined. Nay, the very life of the Lord Jesus—all that He did and said and suffered—was a revelation of the Infinite; for He Himself was God *manifest* in the flesh. And herein is one of the most marvelous methods whereby Jesus Christ was a Revealer of God to man.

But this Great Prophet in Israel is no less familiar with the origin, nature, needs and destiny of man, than He is with all that pertains to God. He knew thoroughly all that was in the heart of man, and had no need that any one should teach Him. He laid bare the deepest recesses of the soul, and solved all those tremendous problems over which man had agonized in vain. The Sermon on the Mount is the most remarkable utterance of truth that was ever heard by mortal man. The more we study this sermon, the readier are we to confess that it far transcends the limit of finite intelligence, and if there were no other proof of His superhuman character, this sermon would for ever establish His claims as a Divine Teacher.

Take the parable of the Rich Man and Lazarus, and where in all the literature of men is so much knowledge of the future world conveyed as in this single parable?

Every parable spoken by Jesus contains a revelation of spiritual truth; and they who have studied most intensely these matchless productions, confess that they have utterly failed to exhaust the richness and depth of instruction contained in them. As a Teacher of men, as a Speaker of parables, as a Revealer of God, the world has never seen such an one as Jesus of Nazareth; no man ever spake as this man.

We call Jesus a Prophet, for so the Evangelists term Him; and He was a Prophet in both uses of the word. A prophet is any one commissioned by God to speak for and from Him to men—the essential idea of the term is not *foretelling* events, as some suppose, but speaking for God to man. There were Prophets who uttered no predictions. But Christ was a Prophet who *foretold* future events; He was a Predictor. Many of His predictions, or prophecies as they are termed, have been left on record; the utter destruction of Jerusalem and the Temple, which was fulfilled to the very letter; the dispersion of the Jews, which is fulfilled in the eyes of men every day that we live; His own death, resurrection and ascension, which were witnessed by hundreds of His countrymen; the progress and establishment of His Church, and the destruction of Satan and his kingdom; the rise of Antichrist, and the restoration of the Jews, and His own glorious advent a second time;—these and many other things were plainly foretold by Him. Some of them have been fulfilled, as we have seen; others are fulfilling now, and others lie still in the future. What we have seen of the past is abundantly sufficient to justify the confident assurance that the future will not fail to vindicate Him as the greatest of all Prophets.

But we are not at liberty to limit the teachings of the God-man to what He Himself uttered. He quotes from the Sacred Books of the Jews; the Law, the Prophets, and Hagiographa, as the Old Testament was classified in His day, and makes Himself responsible for their contents; these writings are His testimony, for the spirit of prophecy is the testimony of Jesus. His Spirit inspired them all, and He, as Teacher and Prophet, is responsible for all.

Besides this, He inspired His Apostles to write other books, and thus to complete the Canon of Scripture; and holy men spake as they were moved by His Spirit. And thus both

Old and New Testament are inspired—theopneustic—God-imbreathed.

When we say that the entire Bible is inspired, it is not meant that every word in that Book is the word of God. Some of the words are the words of the devil; some are the words of wicked men. The Bible is a history; it records the deeds of bad men, the sins of good men, the idolatry of the nations, the apostasies of the Church. It records these things just as they occurred, as facts. But the holy men of old, who wrote these books, were inspired by the Spirit of Jesus to record these facts as a necessary part of the development of the plan of salvation. The religion of Jesus is a religion of facts—it rests upon a historic basis; hence the Spirit of Jesus so directs and controls the minds and pens of the sacred writers, that they select and arrange just the very facts that are necessary to make a complete revelation. Where they record history, the Spirit led them to make the record; where they write proverbs, the Spirit directed them to write proverbs; where they record the predictions of the Prophets, the Spirit bade them record the predictions. It was the Spirit who guided them as to what facts, and proverbs, and psalms, and prophecies should be recorded; and the very form in which the record should be made was also dictated by the same Spirit. For since the truth is conveyed in words, how can that truth be preserved free from any admixture of error unless the form, the words in which the truth is conveyed, is likewise kept free from error? and how can the form be kept free from error unless the Spirit select the words?

All Scripture is *inspired*, but all is not *revealed;* the record of the temptation of Jesus by the devil is an inspired record—the Evangelists wrote as they were moved to write by the Holy Ghost—but there is no revelation in that record. Where Jesus says, God is a Spirit, or where John says, God is love, both of these statements are revelations; they convey truths otherwise unknown to man; and besides being revelations, the statements are inspired—that is, the Spirit moved the writers to record these revelations as part of the Scriptures.

As we examine these holy oracles, what an idea do they give us of the superhuman, the Divine intelligence of the Great Teacher, who directed the composition of them all! The spirit of prophecy, the spirit of the entire Scriptures is a testimony or witness of Jesus; and as we listen to these words we are forced to exclaim, This is the very Christ, the God-man, the Deus-Homo.

CHAPTER V.

The Death of Christ.

THE closing scenes in the lives and the last words of the great and good are matters of profound interest to every thinking man. The interest of a whole life seems gathered and concentrated in the last few moments of the dying man; and all persons seem to think that he who stands upon the confines of the eternal world must speak and act the truth. Concerning the death of Jesus Christ, Rousseau has said: " Socrates lived and died like a sage; Jesus Christ lived and died like a God."

The fact, the time, and the manner of His death were not unknown to the God-man; He had foreseen and foreknown it all long before it came to pass. He had distinctly and repeatedly announced to His disciples that He was to suffer death, and that He was to die at Jerusalem.

The death of Jesus Christ, in whatever aspect

we consider it, was the most remarkable death that has ever occurred among men. Let us gather up the main facts, and endeavor to comprehend their tremendous import. He was put to death in the reign of Cæsar Tiberius, and when Pontius Pilate was Procurator of Judea, then a province of the empire. He was crucified at Jerusalem, and at the time of the old Jewish Feast of the Passover. This Jerusalem was the ancient city of Salem, where Melchizedek, the royal priestly type of Christ, had lived and ruled two thousand years before the Incarnation of the Son of God; it was the old Jebus of the Canaanites; it was the city of the kings of Judah, and it was shrined in the hearts of the Hebrew people by a thousand sacred memories and hallowed associations. It was in every way becoming that Jesus, the Son of David, should suffer in the city of His royal ancestors, the city of His most illustrious type, the city of His own chosen people. He Himself had said, It cannot be that a Prophet perish out of Jerusalem.

There was an eminent propriety, too, in His suffering death at the great Feast of the Passover. This religious festival had been instituted by God Himself more than fifteen hundred years before the death of Jesus Christ. It commemorated the deliverance of the Israelites from their bondage in Egypt, and it pointed them forward to their rest in the Promised Land. The matter of the feast was a male lamb slain; his blood sprinkled upon the lintels of the houses of the Hebrews; the flesh of the lamb cooked, and eaten with bitter herbs and unleavened bread. Now John the Baptist, the forerunner of Messiah, had expressly pointed out Jesus as the Lamb of God that taketh away the sin of the world; and one of the most remarkable of those men who knew Jesus declared that Christ is our Passover, slain for us. The Paschal Lamb appointed of God offers up Himself as a Lamb slain from the foundation of the world, at the time of the Jewish Passover Feast.

Just before the time of the Passover He commanded his disciples to go into the city of Jerusalem, and make ready for them to celebrate the feast and eat the supper. They sat down together to eat His last Passover supper on the earth. While they were partaking of the meal, Jesus took bread, and having given thanks, said: This is my body broken for you; likewise He took the cup, saying, This cup is the New Testament in my blood, which is shed for many for the remission of sins: drink ye all of it; and all who love Him are commanded to eat the bread and drink the wine as a memorial supper, until He shall come a second time, without sin unto salvation.

After they had eaten the Passover, and Jesus had instituted the Lord's Supper, He and His Apostles went unto a place called Gethsemane. This was a garden across the brook Kidron, beyond the limits of the city, and was at the foot of a small mount, called the Mount of Olives. When He reached this garden, He took with Him Peter, James and John, saying to the rest of the disciples, Sit ye here, while I go and pray yonder; and He began to be sorrowful and very heavy. He makes this strange declaration to the three who are with Him—*My soul* is exceeding sorrowful, even unto death; tarry ye here, and watch with me. And now His soul seems to enter into the gloom of a rayless and starless night of sorrow; unutterable agonies seize fast hold upon Him; He begins to speak to some Fourth Person who is invisible to the three; He calls Him Father— Father, if it be possible let this cup pass. He prays to the Invisible to deliver Him in this the hour of His anguish and agony. And then He seems to remember that His great mission into the world was not to do His own, but the will of Him who sent Him, and he exclaims, Nevertheless, not as I will, but as Thou wilt. His sufferings seem to abate somewhat, and He comes to the three; and finding them asleep, gently chides them—Could ye not watch with me one hour? A second time He goes from them and prays to His Heavenly Father—O my Father, if this cup may not pass from me except I drink, Thy will be done. At this point an angel appears from heaven, strengthening Him. Coming again to the three disciples, He finds them asleep; and again He leaves them, and prays the same words. This time He prays more earnestly, and Luke, who was a physician, tells us that His sweat was as it were great drops of blood, falling down to the ground. As He returns the third time to Peter, James and John, a band of armed men with their officers are seen approaching, guided by Judas, one of the Twelve. Judas had been present at the Passover Feast, but had left the little company after Jesus had given him the sop as a token to show who it was that should betray Him. Judas covenanted with the priests to deliver Jesus into their hands for thirty pieces of silver. He now approaches Jesus, saying, Hail, Master! and kisses Him; the kiss was the signal agreed upon, whereby Judas was to indicate to the officers which one of the little company was Jesus. His friends are disposed to resist the arrest, and one of them drew his sword and cut off the ear of the servant of the high priest; but Jesus knowing all things that should come upon Him, steps forth, and says, I am Jesus of Nazareth, whom ye seek. The arrest was made in the night, and the officers carry Jesus at once, before day, to the house of Caiaphas, the high priest.

The preliminary trial of Jesus was held at the house of Caiaphas before day; it was here that Peter so shamefully denied his Lord and Master. When the morning came, He had his *second* examination before the council or Sanhedrim, the highest tribunal of the Jews. The elders and chief priests sought false witnesses against Jesus to put Him to death; but these suborned witnesses did not agree in their testimony; finally the high priest adjured Jesus, by the living God, to tell whether He was the Christ, the Son of God; and Jesus, when thus adjured by the highest officer of the tribunal and nation, declared that He was. The high priest immediately declared that this was blasphemy—that there was no further need of any witness in the case, and demanded of the council, What think ye? The answer was, He is guilty of death.

Nothing was now needed to the execution of the decree of the council except authority from the Roman governor; so the elders, scribes and priests bind Jesus, and carry Him to the hall of Pilate. His *third* trial is before the heathen governor. The charge of blasphemy will avail these bloodthirsty rulers but little in the judgment-hall of Pilate, for Pilate knows nothing of Jehovah, the Jewish God against whom the blasphemy was uttered; and as for the charge of blasphemy, he does not even know the meaning of the word. If, then, these Jewish rulers go into Pilate's court with no other charge against Jesus than this, they will be driven from the judgment-hall. But their malice finds a new and ready charge for the new tribunal to which they have carried the case. We found this fellow perverting the nation —so these Jews, so eminently *loyal* to the Roman empire, affirm—and forbidding to give tribute to Cæsar; saying that He Himself is Christ, a King. Intensely *loyal* are these leaders of the mob ecclesiastical. Their new-born zeal for Cæsar is consuming them, as they see therein a method whereby they may get rid of a religious enemy. In this court the charge is not blasphemy, but treason.

Pilate called Jesus, and said unto Him, Art Thou the King of the Jews? Jesus admitted that He was a king, but affirmed that His Kingdom was not of this world; that if it were, His servants would fight for it; that there was no conflict whatever between Him and Cæsar, between His Kingdom and the empire. Pilate then told the Jews that he found no fault in Christ. This only made them cry out more fiercely against Jesus, declaring that He had stirred up all Jewry, beginning from Galilee. When Pilate heard that He was a Galilean, he determined to send Him to King Herod, who was then in Jerusalem, and to whose jurisdiction Galilee belonged.

His *fourth* examination is before Herod. To the many questions asked Him by Herod, Jesus answered not a word; and then Herod and his men of war set Him at naught, and mocked Him, and arrayed Him in a gorgeous robe of purple, and put on His head a crown of thorns, and sent Him back to Pilate. Pilate said to the Jews, Behold the Man; but they cried out, Crucify Him. Pilate again declares that he finds no fault in Him; and when the Jews declare that by their law He ought to die, because *He made Himself the Son of God*, Pilate is the more afraid and anxious to release Him. But the cry of loyalty to Cæsar terrifies the timid governor, and, washing his hands in water, he brings Jesus forth to the pavement, and said to the Jews, Behold your King—will ye crucify Him? And the frenzied shout of the maddened mob is, Away with Him, crucify Him! we have no king but Cæsar.

It was mid-day when Jesus, bearing His cross, reached the Place of a Skull, called in the Hebrew Golgotha, where He was crucified. Two malefactors are crucified at the same time; the one on the right, the other on the left of Jesus.

As He hangs upon the cross, nature begins to give signs of consternation and woe; the sun shines with pale and sickly rays; darkness begins to gather over the world, until soon it envelops the whole land; the earth, affrighted, quakes with horror; the veil of the temple is rent in twain from top to bottom; the very rocks are burst asunder; the very graves are opened, and the sheeted dead lie exposed; meantime the soul of the Crucified is wrestling with the King of terrors; He is treading the wine-press *alone;* His friends have forsaken Him; and more than all, His Father's face is hid; no angel comes now from the skies to strengthen Him; the ninth hour (three o'clock in the evening) is near at hand; in the intolerable anguish of His spirit, He exclaims, My God, My God, why hast Thou forsaken me? And then, with a loud voice, He cries, It is finished, and gave up the ghost.

The Roman sentinel who witnessed the scene was forced to exclaim, Truly this man was the Son of God.

The death of Christ was the separation of His soul and body. His soul went at once to Paradise, for He said to the penitent thief, To-day shalt thou be with Me in Paradise; His body was laid in the tomb of Joseph of Arimathea.

His death was not caused by the physical pain of the crucifixion, for, just as He died, He cried out with a *loud* voice of triumph; and when the soldiers came to break His legs, they marveled that He was already dead.

But the separation of His soul and body was His own *voluntary act*. He had power to lay down His life, and power to take it up again. His humanity was not descended from Adam by an ordinary generation; but being miraculously formed by the Holy Ghost, was exempted from the death penalty of the law. His life was not taken from Him by violence, for He gave up the ghost. He breathed out His Spirit. He *gave* His life a Ransom for many. His life was His own to give; hence it was not suicide when He breathed out His Spirit.

In His death, the Eternal High Priest offered up His own soul and body as a sacrifice for sin; for His death was in every sense a sacrifice; and He was the Priest who slew and offered the Victim; and He Himself was the Victim. The whole story of His death loses its consistency, and the death itself loses all its efficacy, the moment that you deny His Humanity or His Divinity, or the union of the two natures in the One Person, or the voluntary act of the High Priest in offering the sacrifice.

This is no mere martyr dying for the truth; no mere man just " reeling out of life ;" no mere example of the Perfect Man, to show men how to die ; no mere theatrical display of the method of the Divine government; it is God manifest in the flesh, dying for the sins of the world; it is the Eternal Son, in the likeness of sinful flesh, offering Himself up as a substitute and surety for His own people; it is the Lamb of God taking away the sin of the world. His death is vicarious; it is not for Himself, but for others. He was holy, harmless, undefiled, and separate from sinners, and was not subject to the death-penalty of the law.

He is the High Priest after the order of Melchizedek, offering up the one complete, perfect, and final sacrifice for sin. As God, He could not suffer; as Man, He could not satisfy; but as God-man, as the Deus-Homo, He could both suffer and satisfy. As the Son of God, and as Son of man in One Person, the Person of the God-man, He could offer up Himself, and as such the sacrifice was accepted. In all God's wide domain there was no other life of sufficient worth and dignity to take away sin. Man could offer no human life a sacrifice for sin, for the life of every human being was already forfeited; no angel or seraph could offer for man, for angel and seraph were bound to obey for themselves.

But here is a life that can be given in exchange for the life of man; here is a Priest, with a holy, harmless, undefiled victim; here is a Priest who had no need to offer any sacrifice for Himself; here is a Priest with the power of endless life in Himself, and a Victim with an *unforfeited* life, and this life this Priest voluntarily gives for the lives of others. His death is a priestly offering, a sacrifice, an atonement, a propitiation, a ransom. He gave His life a ransom for many.

When we say that Christ was the substitute for His people, and that He died in their room and stead, and that He who knew no sin was made sin for them, it is not asserted, nor is it meant to teach, that there was any *transfer of moral character*. Of course, the personal moral character of Christ could not be transferred to His people; nor could their personal character be transferred to Him. But there was a transfer of legal obligations—the righteousness of the God-man, wrought out by His obedience and suffering, was transferred, by the act of God the Father, to those for whom Christ obeyed and died: Christ became to them the end of the law for righteousness. The obligation of His people to obey and to suffer was also transferred to Him—their sin was made His, and He bare their sins in His own body on the tree. He was wounded for our transgressions, He was bruised for our iniquities, the chastisement of our peace was upon Him, and with His stripes we are healed; for the Lord hath laid on Him the iniquity of us all.

He who was thoroughly acquainted with the Jewish sacrificial system, he who saw Jesus after his resurrection from the dead, he who of all men was best qualified to unfold the nature of this priestly offering, has left on record his conceptions of the priesthood and sacrifice of the God-man; and as the author of this work is only attempting to present the conception of the God-man as given by His contemporaries, he takes this occasion to introduce the testimony of Paul as given in the Epistle to the Hebrews.

Christ Jesus, he tells us, was superior in nature to the angels; for He was the Son of God, the brightness of His glory, the express Image of His person. He was superior in office to Moses; for Moses was but a faithful servant, while Christ was a faithful Son. He was superior in dignity to Aaron; for His priesthood was after the order of Melchizedek, which was an order of priesthood above the Aaronic. Melchizedek was a real person; he lived two thousand years before Christ; he was king of Salem, and priest of the Most High God. There was no genealogy of his family, no record of his ancestors. History does not tell us who was his father and mother, nor when he began to exercise priestly functions, nor when he died. With the Aaronic order of priesthood the case was different—the genealogy of the family was strictly kept, an accurate pedigree of the priests was preserved; this record stated when each priest entered upon his office and when he ceased to discharge its duties. With Melchizedek the case was otherwise; there was no record, no genealogy; so that, as compared with the Aaronic order, it might be said of him, He was without father, without mother, without descent, having neither beginning of days nor end of life, but made like unto the Son of God, abideth a priest continually.

Jesus Christ, our High Priest, is without mother as to His Divine nature, for that nature had existed long before the Incarnation, and there was no divine mother in the Eternal Trinity : He had been eternally begotten of the Father, and was of the same substance with

Him, and there never had been a time when He was not.

He was without father as to His human nature; for Joseph was only His reputed, not His real father; the Eternal Father was not the father of His human nature, for it was the Holy Ghost, not the Father, that came upon the Virgin; nor is it proper to call the Holy Ghost *father;* because the human body and soul of the man Jesus were *formed*, not begotten of Him: the humanity of Jesus was *formed*, not *generated*.

He was without descent—who shall declare His generation? There had been no one like Him before, and in all time to come there would arise no one like Him. In His wondrous constitution as the Divine-human priest he was isolated and alone in the universe.

Nor with Him was there any beginning of days or end of life; for He was High Priest of an everlasting covenant made in the councils of eternity, before the morning stars had sung together or the sons of God had shouted for joy. Nor has His Priesthood terminated; and it will never end.

The Priesthood of Christ was unchangeable; it never passed from Him to any other person; He had no successor in office. The priests of Levi after the Aaronic order were many, and were not suffered to continue, by reason of death, and the office passed in succession from one to another.

But this Deus-Homo continueth for ever; death has no power to destroy Him or His Priesthood; hence it is unchangeable, it passes to no successor. As His death did not give any occasion for a succession in this office, so after His resurrection He never appointed any successor. The very constitution of His person and the very nature of His priesthood absolutely forbid that there should be any successor to the God-man.

Christ Jesus was made a priest, not after the law of a carnal commandment, but after the power of an endless life. The priests of Levi were appointed in virtue of a carnal commandment—a law concerning the *flesh*. Whoever was descended in the regular line from Aaron, if a male without blemish and thirty years old, belonged to the priestly order: the whole priesthood hung upon a question concerning the flesh, and rested upon the ground of a natural generation. But Christ was priest after the power of an endless life—His life was eternal, uncreated, and higher than the heavens—His life was not derived and dependent; it was original and independent. He had power to lay down His life, and power to take it up again. He had a life that was His own to give, and in Him is life.

The Priesthood and sacrifice of Jesus Christ depend absolutely upon the constitution of the person of the Priest: and the whole story of the Cross becomes an insoluble mystery unless Jesus Christ be indeed the God-man. For how can He, by his own act, separate His soul and body unless He be Divine? and how can He die unless He be human? how can His sufferings satisfy unless He be God? and how can He suffer unless He be man? how can He offer an acceptable sacrifice unless He be a High Priest called of God? and how can the death of the victim secure the life of the sinner, unless the victim have an unforfeited life to substitute for the forfeited life of the sinner? Without the shedding of blood there can be no remission or pardon of sin. Behold the Lamb of God, that taketh away the sin of the world!

CHAPTER VI.

The Resurrection of Jesus.

BEFORE His death, Jesus told his disciples plainly that He would rise from the dead on the third day after His crucifixion; but they understood not what the Resurrection from the dead meant. As He had power to lay down His life, so also He had power to take it up again.

The Pharisees and Priests remembered the words of Jesus, that He would rise upon the third day, and they came to Pilate and asked that the sepulchre should be made sure until the third day, lest his disciples come by night and steal Him away, and say to the people that He is risen from the dead; and the last error be worse than the first. In order to prevent such a deception if it had been possible, the great stone at the mouth of the tomb was sealed and made sure; and a Roman guard was placed at the grave to prevent the disciples from stealing the body of Jesus.

But this was the last thing that suggested itself to their minds; for His crucifixion had dashed to the ground all their high hopes and expectations connected with the restoration of of the kingdom to Israel, and their hearts were sad and nigh to breaking when His corpse was laid in the tomb of Joseph of Arimathea. The Friend whom they loved, the Master whom they served, the Lord whom they followed, and the Saviour whom they adored had passed away from the sight, to be seen, as they supposed, no more by them until the great day. For though He had plainly told them that He would rise from the dead, they did not understand the doctrine of the Resurrection.

On the morning of the third day from His death there was a great earthquake, and the Angel of the Lord descended from heaven and rolled away the stone from the mouth of the sepulchre, and sat upon it. His countenance was like lightning, and his raiment white as snow, and for fear of him the guard did shake and become as dead men. Very early the same morning, certain pious women who were His disciples, Mary Magdalen, and Mary the mother of James, and Salome, came unto the sepulchre at the rising of the sun: to these women, who thus came, the Angel of the Lord, who was seated upon the great stone which he had rolled away from the sepulchre, said, Fear not ye; for I know that ye seek Jesus of Nazareth: He is not here, for He is risen, as He said. Come see the place where the Lord lay.

This was the first knowledge that the disciples had of the Resurrection of Jesus from the dead. It was the first, but it was by no means the only evidence they were to have of the Resurrection of their Lord. For He showed himself alive after His Passion to His followers, by many *infallible proofs*, being seen of them forty days, and speaking to them concerning the things pertaining to the kingdom of God.

I shall make no use in this discussion of the various explicit testimonies and incidental allusions of profane authors as to the general belief among the Jewish people that Jesus had risen from the dead. These testimonies have their use and value; but the grand fact of the Resurrection of Jesus must be established by the writings of his four biographers: if it cannot be established from the writings of the New Testament, it cannot be proved at all.

I assume here, as I have assumed all along, that the books of the New Testament were written by the men whose names they bear, and that these books record events that did actually occur; in other words, these records are trustworthy historic documents. And as nearly all the knowledge we have of Christ and his work is derived from these authors, we must either form our conceptions of Him from these writings, or else confess our utter ignorance of Him and of His work.

As the Resurrection of Jesus is the cornerstone upon which the whole superstructure of Christianity rests, it is well that the proofs of His Resurrection are *infallible*. If Christ be not risen, then the whole system of the Christian religion is false; while, on the other hand, if He is indeed risen, as the angel declared, then that Resurrection carries with it the truth of all that He said and did.

The general statement of the *infallible proofs* is, that during a period of over forty days He was seen alive after His crucifixion by more than five hundred different persons; and these appearances of the risen Jesus were open and unmistakable.

1. The first appearance of Jesus after His Resurrection was to Mary Magdalen, out of whom He had cast seven devils. As she stood at the sepulchre talking with the Angel, she turned herself back and saw Jesus standing, and knew not that it was Jesus; but when He called her by name, she at once recognized the person who addressed her as Jesus of Nazareth, and exclaimed, Rabboni; and she went and told

the disciples that she had seen the Lord and that He had spoken to her.

2. Certain women who had gone to the sepulchre were told by the Angels that Jesus was risen; and as they were returning to Jerusalem to tell the disciples, Jesus met them on the way, saying unto them, All hail; and they came and held Him by the feet, and worshiped Him.

3. The third appearance was to the penitent Apostle Peter. When Cleopas and the other disciple with him, to whom Jesus showed Himself, returned to Jerusalem, they heard the Eleven say, The Lord is risen indeed, and hath appeared unto Simon. This name of Simon was the one by which Peter was usually called by his brethren and by Jesus.

4. The next appearance was to two disciples, one of whom was Cleopas, who were on their way from Jerusalem to Emmaus. As they communed and reasoned by the way, concerning the wondrous events that had so recently occurred in Jerusalem, Jesus drew near and went with them. They narrate some of the facts concerning Jesus of Nazareth; and then declare that certain of their own company, who had gone early that morning to the sepulchre, had not found the body of Jesus, but had seen a vision of angels. Jesus reproves them for

their want of faith, and then, beginning at Moses and the Prophets, He expounded unto them in all the Scripture the things concerning Himself; and when they drew nigh the village he went in with them, and while they sat at meat their eyes were opened and they knew Him.

5. The fifth appearance is to the gathered disciples the evening of the same day, and in Jerusalem. The doors of the room where they were assembled were shut, when suddenly Jesus appeared in their midst, and said, Peace be unto you. It is said of Thomas, one of the followers of Jesus, that He was not with the disciples at this time when Jesus showed Himself unto them.

6. These five appearances of Jesus took place upon the first day of the week, the third day from His crucifixion. One week from this day Jesus showed Himself again to His disciples, who were gathered together upon the Lord's day for his worship. This time Thomas was also present, and he declared that he would not believe in the fact of the Resurrection until he had seen the print of the nails in the hands and the mark of the spear in the side of Jesus. Jesus told him to examine His hands and to thrust his hand into His side, and to be no longer faithless, but believing; and when Thomas saw with his own eyes, and felt with his own

hand he was convinced, and cried out, My Lord, and my God.

7. The *seventh* appearance, if we count the *whole* number—the *third*, if we count the *official* number—was to the *eleven* at the sea of Tiberias. The Apostles, at the suggestion of Simon Peter, had gone fishing; while they were thus engaged Jesus showed Himself unto them, spake to them, gave them bread and fish, and dined with them; and after they had dined, the tender and touching interview narrated by John takes place between the weeping and penitent Peter and his forgiving friend, and Jesus formally reinstates him in the Apostolic College.

8. Jesus appeared again to five hundred brethren at once, some of whom were alive when Paul wrote the Epistle to the Corinthians; for in the fifteenth chapter of that Epistle, treating expressly of the doctrine of the Resurrection, he declares that the Resurrection of Jesus was the foundation of the Christian's hope and immortality; and argues the certainty of the latter from the certainty of Christ's Resurrection; and as one proof that Jesus was risen from the dead, he adduces the fact that five hundred brethren saw Him at one time, of whom the greater part were still alive.

9. Jesus showed himself the ninth time to his brother James.

10. The next appearance was to eleven Apostles at the Mount of Olives near Bethany, when He gave them the Great Commission to go into all the world and preach the Gospel to every creature; and as He finished speaking He was parted from them and ascended up to heaven.

To these ten different and distinct appearances of Jesus must be added His personal appearing to Saul of Tarsus when on his way from Jerusalem to Damascus to persecute the Christians of that city. Jesus showed Himself in His glorified human body to the fierce and bigoted Saul, and said to him, Saul, Saul, why persecutest thou Me? Saul recognized the voice, and knew that the person who spake to him was Jesus of Nazareth.

If any event, natural or supernatural, can be established by human testimony, then, beyond the possibility of a peradventure, Jesus is indeed risen from the dead. If the proofs of any past event be conclusive, then are the proofs of Christ's Resurrection *infallible*. If competent and credible witnesses can establish any fact, then these witnesses do establish the fact of the Resurrection.

There are three, and but three, possible suppositions concerning these witnesses, viz:

First. These witnesses were impostors; they

knew that Jesus was not risen from the dead, and they knowingly deceived the people; or,

Second. They were themselves deceived, and did really believe that Jesus was risen, though he was not; or,

Third. Their testimony is true, and Jesus is indeed risen from the dead.

To suppose that these men were impostors, and they knowingly deceived the people, is to suppose a miracle greater even than the Resurrection of Jesus. For the testimony which they gave was in direct conflict with the opinions and desires of the civil and ecclesiastical authorities; subjecting them on the one hand to the loss of all religious standing among the Jews, and on the other to the loss of civil privileges, and liability to trial for treason, as supporters of a king hostile to Cæsar. If they bore false witness, there were hundreds of men in Jerusalem and Judea to convict them of perjury, and they must suffer the penalty of the Mosaic Law against false swearing; if they still contended that Jesus was King, and that He was risen from the dead, they might suffer any day as their pretended King Jesus had suffered. It is absolutely contrary to human nature, human reason, and human experience that men should propagate falsehoods when they thereby gain nothing, but lose all.

Tradition affirms that all of the Apostles suffered death rather than recant their testimony that Jesus was their risen Lord and King.

And it does seem that any argument to prove that these witnesses were *not* impostors is needless with any man who has ever given their writings a candid perusal. The very character of the evidence given forbids for ever the supposition of imposture or fraud.

But were not these men themselves mistaken? They were good and honest men, and really believed that Jesus was risen, but they were deceived. No one who has ever read the masterly discussions of Paul, or the profound discourses of John, or the logical histories of Luke would ever suppose that these men could be mistaken upon a subject of such vital and transcendent interest and importance as the Resurrection of Him upon whom all their hopes for time and eternity were built.

Suppose that the most prominent man in London were to declare in the presence of hundreds of persons of that city that he would die upon a certain day, and that three days after he would rise from the dead. Suppose his death to occur just as he said it would occur; and that three days after his burial, certain members of his own family, and others of his most intimate friends affirmed most positively that they saw this man alive, talked with him, touched him, and saw certain scars upon his body which were peculiar to him. Suppose the number of those who said they saw him increased day by day, until five hundred and more affirmed that they had seen him. Would not all of this testimony prove that the man was alive from the dead, if human testimony can establish any fact? And if no fact can be established by the testimony of those who saw and heard it, then all knowledge is for ever at end. This thing was not done in a corner; it was open and public. The witnesses who testify to the fact of the Resurrection were of all men the most competent and credible to give true evidence in the case: John had leaned on His bosom; Thomas saw the print of the nails and the mark of the spear; Mary had sat at His feet and had anointed Him for his burial; Peter had been His constant companion; and Paul could never forget what he saw on his way up to Damascus.

The third possible supposition is the true one: these men are true witnesses, competent and credible, and Jesus is indeed risen from the dead.

The Nature of Christ's Resurrection.

Christ, in the beautiful language of inspiration, was the First-fruits of them that slept; and in His Resurrection and Gospel He has brought Life and Immortality to light.

There had been traces and types of the resurrection of the dead and the life everlasting long before Jesus appeared to His followers in His glorified human body. The germs of this sublime doctrine are found in the Old Testament Scriptures—a doctrine revealed by God, at sundry times and in diverse manners in time past, to the Fathers, but now revealed unto us by His Son, whom He hath appointed Heir of all things.

Enoch, the seventh from Adam, lived three hundred and sixty and five years, and Enoch walked with God, and was not, for God took him; that is, he was translated to heaven and did not see death.

The Angel of the Lord appeared unto Moses out of the midst of a bush, and though the bush burned with fire, yet the bush was not consumed; and God spake unto Moses, saying, I am the God of Abraham, of Isaac, and of Jacob. Fifteen hundred years after, Jesus expounded this very Scripture to the Sadducees, who denied the doctrine of the Resurrection of the dead; Ye do err, said he, not knowing the Scripture or the power of God; have ye not read that which was spoken unto you by God, saying, I am the God of Abraham, of Isaac, and of Jacob. These men were dead when God spake these words; how then could He be their God? But though they had died, yet still they were alive; for God is not the God of the *dead*, but of the *living*.

Elijah, the Prophet of the Lord, who confronted Ahab, Jezebel, and the priests of Baal, was taken up from before the very eyes of his Elisha to heaven in a chariot of fire and with horses of fire.

There are three cases recorded in the Gospels where the dead were brought back to life, to complete in the flesh their mortal existence.

The daughter of Jairus had died, and was laid out upon her bed prepared for her burial; and all her friends and relatives wept and bewailed her. Jesus, taking with Him Peter, James, and John, went into the room, and said unto her, Maid, arise: and her spirit came again, and she arose straightway.

A widow of Nain lost her only son, and the funeral procession was carrying the young man on his bier to the grave when Jesus met them, and came and touched the bier, and the dead sat up and began to speak.

The third case is still more remarkable. The first was raised from the bed whereon she had died; the second was raised from the bier whereon he was carried to the grave; the third was raised from the grave wherein he was laid.

Lazarus, the friend of Jesus and the brother of Martha and Mary, had been buried four days when Jesus reached Bethany, where the sisters resided; but when Jesus stood at the grave and said, Lazarus, come forth, the sheeted and stinking dead came to life again, and arose and came forth and was restored to his friends.

It is to be specially noted that in these three instances there was no change wrought in the persons who were raised from the dead; they were in all respects precisely the same after as before their resurrection; they were restored to a purely natural life, and lived in the same manner after their return to a mortal existence that they had lived before their death; and then they all died again and returned to dust, where their bodies now await the Resurrection morning, when at the sound of the Archangel's trump their bodies shall be made like unto Christ's glorious body.

Christ's Resurrection differs from these in this, that His human body was changed and glorified: with Him the mortal put on Immortality, and the corruptible Incorruption.

His human body was changed, but he preserved His identity; He was the same Jesus after His Resurrection that He was before. His beloved friends all recognized Him as the same —the gentle Mary, the loving John, the impetuous Peter, the skeptical Thomas, all knew Him to be the same Jesus they had known before His crucifixion. Nay, so complete was the identity that the marks of the nails and the spear were plainly visible upon His body. It is true the body was changed, immortalized, glorified, but it preserved intact its identity.

His body, like every other human body, had been sown in weakness; it had been raised in power. Before His death Jesus had been subject to all the weakness of humanity, sin of course excepted; He hungered and thirsted, and needed sleep and rest, just as other men. His body was subject to the same laws of time and space that govern other human bodies; but after His Resurrection all these weaknesses of humanity disappear, nor is His body any longer subject to the laws of time and space; for in a moment He would appear all of a sudden to His disciples, and then as suddenly He was gone. On one occasion, when the eleven were gathered in Jerusalem, with the door fastened for fear of the Jews, He appears instantly in their midst without the door being opened.

Although thus changed, He was still the same Jesus; and to convince His affrighted followers that He was not a mere disembodied Spirit returned from the realms of shade, He showed them His hands and feet, and told them to handle Him and see for themselves; and then added that a disembodied spirit did not have flesh and bones as He had.

Many persons conceive of the Resurrection state as one purely spiritual, and of heaven as a rest and home for disembodied spirits; whereas the risen and glorified bodies have part in the Resurrection state, and heaven is the local habitation of both the bodies and spirits of the Just made perfect. It is true that the natural body is changed and fitted for spiritual purposes, is made like unto Christ's own glorious body, and is thus prepared for the mansions of the blest.

Another change wrought in the body of Jesus was that it became immortal. The death of the body was a part of the penalty for the violation of the Divine law—In the day that thou eatest thereof thou shalt surely die; and this sentence of a broken covenant and a violated law had passed upon every son and daughter of Adam for four thousand years, with the exceptions of Enoch and Elijah, who were translated that they should not taste death.

The God-man, speaking in the person of His great Type one thousand years before, said: Thou wilt not leave my soul in Hades; neither wilt Thou suffer thine Holy One to see corruption; and the Apostle Peter upon the day of Pentecost, speaking upon the fact of the Resurrection of Jesus, declared that His soul was not left in Hades, and that *His flesh did not see corruption*. This is the only particular wherein the Resurrection of Jesus differs from that of His brethren. The bodies of believers moulder into dust and *see corruption*: Christ's body did *not* moulder, neither did it *see corruption*.

And the reason of this is to be found in the fact that Jesus was begotten and born not after the manner of ordinary generation, but by the direct agency and power of the Holy Ghost. His human body was superhumanly *formed* by the Third Person of the Godhead in the womb of the Virgin, and of her substance; pollution was not therefore transmitted in the regular channel of generation, and as it could not, in the nature of the case, be imputed, the body of Jesus was not subject to corruption. Nor could He die an ordinary death in a natural way as the penalty of violated law; but He must Himself lay down His life in virtue of His own power over life. This commandment He had received of His Father.

But, though it did not see corruption, an immortal change passed upon His body. A similar change had passed upon it on the Mount of Transfiguration, when the cloud overshadowed Peter, James, and John, and when Moses and Elias appeared with Jesus, when the fashion of His countenance was altered, and His raiment became white and glistening. This was to show the nature of that Transfiguration which will pass upon the righteous who are alive at His second coming.

When He rose from the grave His body, which had been sown in weakness, was raised in power; sown in dishonor, it was raised in glory: the mortal put on immortality, and the Resurrection body of the Son of Man was powerful, honorable, glorious, incorruptible, and immortal.

And when the Son of Man comes a second time, He will come in this same glorified human nature.

The death of Christ took away the curse and condemnation of the law—the Resurrection secures the pardon and acceptance of believers.

The Resurrection of Jesus secures the Resurrection of all who believe in Him, and is a type of their Resurrection; their bodies shall be made like unto His own glorious body.

I am the Resurrection and the Life; he that believeth in Me, though he were dead, yet shall he live. If we believe that Jesus died and rose again, even so them also that sleep in Jesus will God bring with Him. He that raised up Christ from the dead shall also quicken your mortal bodies by His Spirit that dwelleth in you. Christ is the Head, believers are the body, and where the Head is there shall the body be also. They who believe in Jesus need not fear the grave, for it cannot hold them in its cold embrace; the sting is taken from death, and the victory from the grave, by Him who rose from both. As Lazarus came forth when Jesus called, so shall also all who love Jesus come forth at His appearing and His kingdom.

But if Christ be not risen from the dead, then is the Christian religion vain, and they also that are fallen asleep in Jesus are perished; but now is Christ risen from the dead, and become the First-fruits of them that slept; and as in Adam all die, so in Christ shall all be made alive; but every man in his own order or class.

All that sleep in the dust shall awake—some to everlasting life, some to shame and everlasting contempt; they that be wise shall shine as the brightness of the firmament, and they that turn many to righteousness as the stars for ever and ever. The hour is coming when the dead shall hear the voice of the Son of God, and they that hear shall live.

Many current conceptions of the Resurrection state and the Life everlasting are far more obscure and unsatisfactory than they ought to be; for if Christ's Resurrection be a type of the Christian's Resurrection, then the future state of the righteous is no dim, vague, unreal life of disembodied spirits, but a real and palpable life of glorified humanity.

The life and immortality brought to light in the Gospel by the Resurrection of Jesus from the dead is a life of purified, quickened, and glorified humanity; it is an immortality of mortality. All that is noble, and true, and pure, and lofty, and good in the life here on earth will be transferred to the world beyond the grave, to the land across the Jordan. The identical man will live on in a better country; he will preserve his self-conscious existence and all the blessed memories of the life he now lives.

It is this sublime doctrine that lays at the basis of any comfortable hope concerning our beloved dead. When the Lord shall descend from heaven with the voice of the archangel, we which are alive and remain shall be caught up with all the righteous and risen dead to meet the Lord in the air, and to be for ever with and for ever like Him; wherefore comfort one another with these words, and let not the living righteous sorrow for their righteous dead as those who have no hope.

There will be a grand gathering of all God's righteous dead on the morning of the Resurrection; for their dead dust is precious in His eyes who is the Resurrection and the Life, and those eyes are keeping loving watch over all that precious dust till the trump of God shall wake the dead. No matter where the saint dies, nor where he is buried, that body and that grave are known to Him who never slumbers or sleeps. Jesus watches over all the lonely graves and all the scattered dust of His dear people; and Moses, and Paul, and Polycarp, and Wycliffe, and Knox, and Luther, and Bunyan, and Patriarchs and Prophets, and Apostles and Martyrs, and they of whom the world was not worthy, they who perished on the deserts, and they who went down to the bottom of the deep, they who sleep in the old family burial-place, and they who were slain in battle, and all the bodies of the dear little children who have laid them down to sleep,—these, oh! all these, will Jesus bring with Him on the morning of the Resurrection.

That will be the grandest assembly the Universe ever saw, when the righteous and risen dead, gathered from all lands and kindreds and tribes and people, shall be caught up in the air to meet the Lord, and to be with Him for ever. Blessed and holy and happy is he who shall have part in *this*, the First Resurrection, for the wicked dead rise not until the thousand years are ended.

CHAPTER VII.

The King and His Kingdom.

THE great difficulty with the people was, how to reconcile the apparently conflicting elements in the person, life, and work of Jesus Christ. How could the carpenter of Nazareth, the Son of Mary, teach with such superhuman wisdom and such Divine authority? How could David's son be at the same time David's Lord? How could He work such miracles, and yet be a blasphemer, claiming equality with God? How could the Son of God die? and how could the Son of Man rise from the dead? This was the stone of stumbling and the rock of offence. And to this day, this is the difficulty with Rationalistic conceptions of the life and work of Jesus.

Reason recognizes Him as human, the Son of Man, the Son of Mary; but, refusing to see that while He was human He was also Divine, the Son of the Highest as well as the Seed of the woman, it has utterly failed to grasp or present the true conception of the Christ of history, the Christ of God.

Nowhere was the difficulty greater than to reconcile His regal claims with His lowly station. How can this man, without throne, or crown, or court, or sceptre, or legions, or kingdom, be a king? But He was, nevertheless, a king; yea, the King of kings, and Lord of lords. A king, and, though men saw it not, a king with throne, and crown, and court, and sceptre, and legions, and kingdom.

He was a king by *birth;* for He was of the Royal House of David on His human side, and on the Divine side He was the First-born of the Eternal King. And the question asked by the wise men of the East was, Where is He that is *born* king of the Jews; for we have seen His star in the East, and have come to worship Him; and though His dwelling-place was a stable, and His cradle a manger, yet the wise men worshiped Him as King; and His name was Wonderful, Counsellor, Mighty God, Prince of Peace.

Born a King, He also *died* a King. The charge upon which He was tried was, that He claimed to be Christ, a King. The soldiers platted a crown and placed it upon His head, and bowed the knee to Him, saying, Hail, King of the Jews. When Pilate asked Him if

He was a King, He confessed and denied not that He was. Pilate's question to the Jews was, Shall I crucify your King? The very superscription placed over His head on the cross, written in the three great languages of the world—the Hebrew, the Greek, and Latin—was Jesus of Nazareth, the King of the Jews; and thus the heathen Governor, in the exercise of his own free agency, was unconsciously registering, for the reading of the whole race, the eternal decree of Jehovah, when He set the Messiah Jesus as King upon His holy hill of Zion. As King He died upon the cross, conquering Satan and Hell, and crying with a loud voice, It is finished.

And so, too, it was in virtue of His kingly office and kingly power, that having as High Priest laid down His life, He now took up that life again, and rose triumphant from the grave; for it was not possible that such a King could be holden of it.

As King, He ascended up on high, leading captivity captive, escorted by the great cloud of Angels; and for Him, as King of glory, the everlasting doors were lifted up, and the Lord strong and mighty entered through the pearly gates, and sat down upon His Mediatorial Throne.

And now He reigns as King in heaven and

on earth; He rose from the grave to sit as Prince and Saviour at God's right hand, to give repentance unto Israel and the Remission of sins. He is exalted far above all Principalities and Powers, and is Head over all things to the Church and for the Church, which is His kingdom.

And when He returns to earth, as He most assuredly will, He will then appear in glory, as the mighty King of Zion, with thousands and tens of thousands of Angels, to execute judgment upon His enemies, to deliver His people, and to inaugurate the Millennial reign.

In all His life, and in all His work, in His birth, in His death, in Resurrection, in His exaltation, in His second Advent, He is King—King of kings and Lord of lords. He is King by birthright, King by inheritance, King by nature, King by the oath and gift of Jehovah, King by conquest, King by purchase. In all the universe there is no such King—in all the universe no such kingdom.

The God-man receives and holds His kingdom as the *gift* of His Eternal Father; the crown is placed upon the Son's head by Him who is the Sovereign Lord of the whole Creation. Saith Jehovah, I have set my King upon my holy hill of Zion; ask of Me, and I will *give* Thee the heathen for Thine inheritance, and the uttermost parts of the earth for a possession. By the act of God He was constituted Mediator of the Covenant of Grace, and as the reward of His obedience and suffering under that Covenant, God the Father *gave* Him the kingdom. The kingdom results from the Covenant, is the outgrowth of the Covenant; and all those whom the Father gave the Son are members of the kingdom. There is no room for any doubt as to the reality or nature of the Covenant; for the King Himself says, I have manifested Thy name unto the men that Thou gavest me out of the world; Thine they were, and Thou gavest them Me. I pray not for the world, but for them Thou hast given Me; all that the Father hath given Me shall come unto Me, and him that cometh I will in no wise cast out.

The God-man here speaks of a certain definite, fixed number of persons given Him in some past time by the Father. He declares that all those thus given will be sure to come unto Him; and His purpose is elsewhere declared to keep them by His own power, through faith unto salvation.

It was because the Son of God took upon Him the form of a servant, and became obedient unto death, even the death of the cross, that God also hath highly exalted Him, giving Him a name that is above every name; that at the name of Jesus every knee should bow, and every tongue should confess that He is King, to the glory of God the Father.

Most of the kings of the earth hold their kingdoms by the right of *conquest*. One king goes to war with another king, and having a stronger army, and wiser generals, and greater resources, and a richer treasury, he overcomes the second king, and takes from him part of his possessions, and annexes them to his own crown.

Christ is a King also by right of *conquest*. He spoiled the powers of darkness, and wrested man from the grasp of the destroyer. Satan was the God of this world, and the family of man were his willing subjects. They had renounced their allegiance to God and had transferred their affections to Satan. He was the strong man armed, who kept his house and goods, but a stronger than he came upon him and entered his house and took his goods. The Prince of the power of the air had no right to these goods, to this dominion over man. He had deceived man; he was a liar and a murderer; his dominion was a usurped dominion; and his only claim upon man was a claim founded in deceit and force and fraud.

But still he had power over man, and his kingdom of darkness was a terrible reality, and men were led captive by him at his will. The chains wherein he held his subjects were light, but they were made of burnished steel, and man could not break them. His dominion was a usurpation; but, like all usurpers, he ruled with a rod of iron.

Into this kingdom of darkness the God-man entered, and with this foul Spirit, the King of Zion grappled. The yoke of bondage upon the necks of those given him in the everlasting Covenant must be broken, and His people must be made willing in the day of His power. As second Adam, as Mediator of an Eternal Covenant, as King in Zion, the God-man undertakes to destroy him who held this usurped dominion, and to deliver them who through fear of death were all their life long subject to this bondage.

The struggle was fierce and bitter and bloody, the matter in dispute could not be compromised; and any truce was impossible from the very nature of the case.

In the death grapple, the Captain of our Salvation was made perfect through suffering, and though the Son of God, yet learned He obedience by His very sufferings.

The conflict culminated on Calvary; the God-man died in fearful agony upon the cross; but in the very hour and article of death He triumphed as a King most gloriously, and exclaimed with a loud voice, It is finished; and then He saw Satan as lightning falling from heaven. By dying Himself, He saves those whom the Father gave Him from eternal death, and snatches them as brands from the everlasting burning. As He had power to lay down His life, so He had power to take it up again; and when He took up the life that He had laid down, and rose from the dead, then indeed were His people free, and Satan's usurped dominion broken.

The God-man, having spoiled Satan and having broken the yoke of bondage, makes His people willing in the day of His power, translates them out of the kingdom of darkness into the marvelous light of His own glorious kingdom, subdues His and their enemies under His feet, and rules over and reigns in His willing subjects.

Sometimes, kings acquire possessions not by gift, nor by inheritance, nor by conquest, but by purchase; and Christ is also King by right of *purchase:* His kingdom is His *purchased* possession; the church of God is *bought* with His own blood. His subjects are redeemed not with silver or gold, or any such perishable thing, but with His own precious blood.

Of course, there is no such doctrine of this kingdom, as that so much blood was given for just so many souls; that had there been less blood or less agony, there had been fewer souls saved. This is not the doctrine taught by the King; but He does teach that He paid a *price* for His kingdom, and that price was His own blood. There was a debt due to the law—a debt of obedience and a debt of suffering. The debt was justly due; and the law could not say that it was not due, nor could the law cancel the debt; for the moment it did that, the law ceased to exist, and the law, which was holy, just, and good, could not commit suicide. The debt, then, must be paid. But may not the Substitute pay the debt due from the principal? May not Christ obey and suffer for His people? May He not thus redeem and purchase them?

Man was debtor to the law, and he was in prison, and could by no means come out until he had paid the very last farthing: the God-man comes forward, assumes the payment of the debt, and the prisoner is released; henceforward he must serve his new Master.

This payment of the sinner's debt was not a mock transaction, a mere sham; it was a *bona fide* purchase, and the price was paid in *legal tender* currency; not silver or gold, it is true, but something far more precious, even the blood of Jesus Christ, as of a Lamb slain from the foundation of the world.

This Jesus of Nazareth is, then, a King—King by investiture from the Sovereign of the worlds, King by right of conquest, and King by right of purchase. Who, then, will dare deny His royal claims and character? Behold the Man, the King!

CHAPTER VIII.

The Structure of Christ's Kingdom.

THE Christian Church is the kingdom of the God-man; it bears His name, and is His purchased possession.

However much men dispute as to who and what Christ was, or whether any such person ever lived or not, there can be no dispute as to the fact that the Christian Church does exist. It exists as an outward visible Institute among men; it must have had some origin, and it must owe allegiance to some King. It is to-day a living organization; and it can be traced back historically to the time when Christ lived and taught.

If men reject the account of this kingdom given by the writers of Sacred history, then they must give some satisfactory explanation of its origin; the fact of the existence of this kingdom must be accounted for.

This Christian Church, through all its rulers and all its members, claims to have been founded by Christ, whose name it bears, and it owns Him as rightful King and Lord.

The fact that the Christian Church has survived all the efforts made to destroy it is a most instructive commentary on its supernatural origin and structure. For eighteen centuries, its life has been assailed by the fierce fires of persecution from without, and the fiercer fires of apostasy from within; and yet it has lived to see the death of all who dared to attempt the destruction of its God-given existence. It lives to-day, and it will live when all its enemies are dead.

The Scriptures give the only satisfactory solution of the continued existence of the Church; it was built by the God-man, and it is founded upon the God-man as chief corner-stone.

When Simon Peter, in answer to the question of Christ, Whom say ye that I am? said, Thou art the Christ, the Son of the Living God; the reply from the Son of God was, Upon this confession, that I am the Son of God, I will build my Church, and the gates of hell shall not prevail against it. The Church, then, rests upon Christ as a foundation; and when the rains descend, and the floods come, and the winds blow, it is no wonder that a house resting upon such a Rock should stand.

The Church rests upon an invisible, absent

King. This remarkable fact is pointed out with great clearness and power by the first Napoleon when a prisoner upon St. Helena. In a conversation with General Bertrand, he demonstrates the Divinity of Jesus Christ, and then goes on to show the difference between the kingdom founded by Christ, and all other kingdoms founded by men.

"I have so inspired multitudes," said the great Emperor, "that they would die for me. But, after all, my presence was necessary—the lightning of my eye, my voice, a word from me. Now that I am at St. Helena, now that I am alone, chained upon this rock, who fights and wins empires for me? Who thinks of me? Who makes efforts in Europe for me? Such is the fate of great men. So it was with Cæsar and Alexander.

"Can you conceive of a dead man making conquests, with an army faithful and entirely devoted to his memory? My armies have forgotten me even while living, as the Carthaginian army forgot Hannibal. Can you conceive of Cæsar from the depths of his mausoleum governing the Roman Empire? But such is the history of the conquest of the Christian Church, such is the power of the God of Christians. Whose is the arm which for eighteen hundred years has protected the Church from so many storms which have threatened to engulf it?"

The problem of the Christian Church is solved when we remember that it is founded upon the God-man, and built by the God-man.

I will build my Church, said the Son of the Living God. There is heard no sound of any human axe or hammer in this wondrous structure, this kingdom and house of the God-man. It is the hand of the Deus-Homo that selects and prepares and places every stone in this Spiritual Temple.

The Divine Man left no part of this house to be built by His followers, the members of His kingdom; He Himself built and furnished the whole, and left to His subjects a complete and finished kingdom. He gave it a written Constitution under which it exists; He gave it a complete system of Doctrine which the Church must proclaim; He instituted a Government which the Church must administer, and a Worship which the Church must observe. Every office-bearer in this kingdom is appointed by Him, whether Apostle, or Prophet, or Evangelist, or Pastor, or Teacher, or Elder, or Deacon. Every sacrament to be administered in this kingdom must stand in virtue of His kingly command. Every act of worship or government must be performed in the manner pointed out by the King. Absolutely nothing is left to the invention of man. It is Christ who gives the Sacraments, and the Sabbath, and the Spirit, and the Word, the Doctrine, the Rulers and the Courts—all, all is from the God-man; and He is Head and King over all.

The Constitution of the Christian Church is fixed by the King in Zion, and is unalterable save by the King Himself; and the Doctrine, the Worship, and the Government of the kingdom are to be sought for and found only in the written Constitution, the word of God, which is the complete Statute Book of the kingdom.

The God-man, as the Teacher of men, hath revealed a doctrine, and inspired holy men of old to commit the same to writing for the future instruction and guidance of the members of His kingdom. The word of God, which is contained in the Scriptures of the Old and New Testament, is the *only* rule to the Church of what doctrine she is to believe and teach; for all Scripture is given by inspiration of God, and is profitable for doctrine; therefore the command is, Preach the Word. The doctrine to be believed and taught by the Church is complete and perfect. The Canon of doctrine is closed; the sayings of the prophecy of the God-inspired Book are ended and sealed. If now any man shall add unto the doctrines of the kingdom, God shall add unto him every plague written in the Book; if any man shall take from the doctrines of the Book, God shall take away his part out of the Book of Life, and out of the Holy City, and from the things that are written in this Book.

There are to be no more Revelations from heaven, until the King Himself is revealed in flaming fire, gathering His elect and taking vengeance on His enemies. If, now, men come telling of new Revelations made from heaven by spirit-rappings or dealings with the dead, go not after them; if they come telling of new Words of God found in lonely places, believe them not.

Whatsoever truth the Royal Teacher hath revealed the Church must proclaim—where He hath not spoken the Church dare not speak. She must not go beyond the commandment of the Lord, to say or to do, either good or bad. What the King hath said, that and only that must she proclaim.

There is no place in this kingdom for the traditions of Elders or Apostles; for the commandments of men; for the opinions of Councils; for the bulls of the Pope;—all must be of faith, derived from the Word of the King, and standing in the power of the God-man.

The doctrine is so perfect and complete that everything not contained explicitly or implicitly in the Statute Book of the kingdom is utterly excluded from the Faith and Practice of the Church.

As the Divinely-appointed Custodian of the Truth, the Church must not *make*, she must *proclaim*, the doctrines revealed by the Head of the kingdom. She has no authority to make any doctrine for the King.—He is the only doctrine-maker.

Ye are *witnesses* of these things, teaching them to observe all things whatsoever I have commanded. Clearly enough, the Church is limited, both by her constitution and commission, to teaching the things contained in the Statute Book of the kingdom. Questions of civil allegiance, political tenets, dividing inheritances, in short, all that is secular, must be handed over to the tribunals of Cæsar. For where the Law of the kingdom is silent, the Church has no opinion to give. In fact, she has no business uttering *opinions* of any sort.—Her work is not with opinions, but with *authoritative truth*.

If any set of religious teachers, or any church, or even any angel, come among you, claiming to act by authority from Christ, and proclaim any other truth than that found in the old Statute Book of the kingdom, whether it be the new Evangel of Cæsar, or Loyalty, or Freedom, or Reform, let him be anathema: to the Law and the Testimony of the God-man—if his servants speak not according to these, then let them be cast out as usurpers of the King's prerogatives.

Not to express human opinions, not to make terms of Christian communion, not to legislate for Christ, but to proclaim the finished system of Doctrine, to preach the Word, and expound the Statute Book and Laws of the kingdom, was the work given to the Church by Him who is both her Lord and Law-giver.

Men speak of the "*legislative powers*" of the Church, but from whom did she ever receive one particle of authority to make laws for that kingdom which is universal and eternal? In such a kingdom as this, the King, not the subject, makes laws. Every law having any binding obligation in the Church must be promulgated by the King in Zion.

It is not strange that the American Church, failing to comprehend the Structure of the kingdom of Heaven, and failing to comprehend the limitations of her commission, has departed so far and so sadly from her province and functions, as fixed by Him who gave her the *keys* of the kingdom of Heaven.

The Church, besides, being from her very structure, a Teaching Institute, is also a Worshiping Institute.—She not only proclaims the Doctrines of the kingdom, she must worship the King.

When Moses received the oracles of God, prescribing the Worship of the Lord, he was commanded, See that thou make all things after the pattern shown thee in the mount; and the heaviest curses of the Law are denounced against him who shall add to or take from the prescribed worship of the kingdom.

Under the Ancient Dispensation, the worship was ritualistic and sensuous, but still appointed of God, a shadow of good things to come. Under this dispensation, the worship is purely spiritual—the hour is now come, when neither in this mountain, nor yet at Jerusalem, shall the Father be worshiped. God is a Spirit, and they who worship Him must worship in spirit and in truth; for He desireth a spiritual worship.

All things pertaining to His worship, not enjoined by the King, are not merely *indifferent*, they are *sinful;* and it were well if this great principle of the kingdom, as practiced in Apostolic days, and as held by all the Reformed Church, were more distinctly enunciated and more faithfully enforced in this day of Will-worship and Apostasy.

The Doctrines of the kingdom relate more especially to the Prophetic office of the God-man—the worship relates more especially to His priestly work; as High Priest, He slays the victim as a solemn act of worship; as Priest, He opens up a new and living way of access to God; as Priest, He goes into the very presence of the Father, with sacrificial blood in His hands, interceding for His people. In the nature of the case, the High Priest will not sprinkle with His atoning blood, and present to the Father, the prayers and oblations of His people, unless they be such as He has prescribed, and unless they be presented in the manner pointed out by Him.

Plainly enough, there is no place and no authority in this kingdom for any Ritual-making —the Royal Priest is the only Ritual-maker. Hence the folly and sin of all those attempts— no matter, by whomsoever made—to render the simplicity and spirituality of the worship, as appointed by the God-man, more acceptable to the carnal mind and heart by human devices and inventions of men. To all those who would improve the worship of the kingdom in ways and by methods not commanded by Christ, the ready question suggests itself, Who hath required this at your hands?

A third essential element in the structure of this kingdom is the power of Rule or Government. A kingdom cannot exist without law, and law unexecuted is no law. It seems the height of folly to suppose that the God-man built a kingdom that was to outlive all kingdoms, and yet appointed no Government for His subjects; that He revealed a Doctrine and prescribed a Worship, but ordained no Government.

The Government is upon His shoulders; and every Ruler is called and appointed by Him, and every Court or Council of the kingdom sits in His name and acts by His authority. When He ascended on high He gave every gift that the Church possesses; and all of these gifts are for the express purpose of perfecting the saints, the work of the ministry, and the edifying of the body of Christ.

How absurd the folly of all those who undertake to form a better government for this kingdom than that framed by the King Himself! And yet the Church has always been afflicted with *government-makers.*

These government-makers went upon the theory, that the old government given by the King, through Patriarchs, Prophets, and Apostles was at best incomplete; or even if adapted to the olden times, still, with the increased light and advanced thought of this day, it was inadequate to meet the exigencies of the present demands.

Some even denied that Christ as King had ever established any government for His kingdom, but affirmed that He had left the whole matter of Rule to be fixed by the members of

His kingdom as the varying circumstances of the times demanded; or, at the best, the King had only incidentally enacted a few general principles of government, and had left His people at liberty to develop these principles and to arrange all details; that when the God-man founded a kingdom and built a house, there was no Divine plan and no *finished* work.

Utterly ignoring the kingly office and Headship of Christ, and the divinely-appointed officebearers, courts and instrumentalities of the Church, they have devised, in the wisdom of men, scores of schemes for doing the work of Christ's kingdom; hence come voluntary societies, Christian Commissions, Christian Associations, Board of Missions, and other human machinery; hence, too, the doctrine that the Pope, or Cæsar, or somebody else is king.

Surely, after the robes and sceptre and crown are taken from the God-man, some other king must be found to wear and wield them. After the dethronement of Christ, the King, there may be an interregnum, but no longer shall the interregnum last than a new king can be found or made. Cæsar is the most popular candidate for regal honors, now-a-days, in that kingdom which is not of this world. And woe to both Church and State when he takes his seat upon the Mediatorial Throne!

The Structure of Christ's Kingdom. 127

The kingdom of the God-man is then a *finished* and perfect structure. Its doctrine is revealed; its worship is prescribed; and its government is instituted—nothing, as pertaining to Doctrine, Worship or Government, is left to the devices of man. The God-man *completed* everything, and left to His followers no functions or powers of kingdom-building whatever.

The foregoing statements must be qualified by the following limitation, viz.: There are some things *common* to all kingdoms, all societies, all organizations, all assemblies; those things that are common flow from the very nature of the kingdom, society, or assembly, and are necessary and unavoidable. If a revealed doctrine is to be proclaimed, it must be proclaimed from some *place;* if a prescribed worship is to be observed, it must be observed at some *hour* of the day; if the divinely-appointed office-bearers of the kingdom meet in assemblies, there must be a *presiding officer.* These and other things that are common to all organizations and assemblies are not built into the kingdom, but are to be ordered by Christian people, in accordance with the injunction, Let everything be done decently and in order. These things, without which, the doctrine could not be proclaimed, the worship observed, and the government administered, are not a part of the structure built by the God-man, but flow from the very nature of the structure; these things are not fixed by the King, but they are the only things not fixed by Him.

Whatever power, therefore, the Church may have, must be a *derived* power—must come from the God-man, as Teacher, Priest and King. It is a power declarative and ministerial—the power of a herald to declare the will of the King; the power of a servant to do the will of the Master; the power to declare the mind of the King as contained in the Statute Book of the kingdom; the power to administer the affairs of the Church in accordance with the Laws of the kingdom.

Her's is the Power of the keys—to open and to shut the doors of the kingdom. Whatsoever the Church binds on earth in His name, by His authority, and in accordance with His revealed will, is bound in heaven: and so in like manner with whatsoever the Church shall loose on earth.

But the question arises just here, How is the kingdom of the God-man to be distinguished from other kingdoms?

There are false prophets and false Christs; and there are false Churches and apostate Churches. But if we bear in mind the structure of Christ's Church, we will have very little difficulty in indentifying the kingdom not of this world.

As this kingdom is spiritual and supernatural, founded upon Christ, and built by Christ, with a revealed doctrine, a prescribed worship, and an ordained government, and as the Record of all this is contained in the Scriptures of the Old and New Testament, it is perfectly obvious that the man who starts to find the *true Church must commence his search with the Bible in his hand*. For as the King in Zion describes the Church in His Revealed Will, it is evident that every true Church will correspond with His description. But Doctrine, Worship and Government cover the totality of the life of the Church. Here, then, are the infallible marks:

1. Any Church that proclaims the Doctrine revealed by the King,

2. Any Church that Worships God after the manner pointed out by the King,

3. Any Church that maintains the government set up by the King—is a true Church of Jesus Christ, is part of the kingdom of the Godman.

Any arrogant and exclusive claim set up by any body of men to be the true Church is, in its very nature, presumptuous. The claim to be the true Church must be substantiated by a correspondence with the description given by the

King. The Church must possess the essential features of the structure built by Christ, or it is no part of His heritage. These marks are so few and simple that no man, with the Word of the King in his hands, need make any mistake as to the kingdom of the God-man.

There is a *fourth* mark, or rather there is a test of the marks already given, viz.: Holiness of Life. By their fruits ye shall know them, is a universal test. The invariable result of true doctrine, spiritual worship and scriptural government is holiness of heart and life; and wherever holiness is found in connection with scriptural doctrine, worship and rule, there is the true kingdom of the God-man.

There may be departures to some extent in the particulars of doctrine, worship and government, and the Church may still be a true, though very imperfect Church; but beyond a certain point these departures cannot go without the Church becoming apostate.

This kingdom of the God-man is His perpetual representative among men. As His servants and subjects proclaim the finished doctrines of the kingdom, they exalt the Great Teacher sent from God; as they order and observe the spiritual worship prescribed in the laws of the kingdom, they glorify the Great High Priest; as they recognize the Headship and kingly office of the Son of the Living God, and maintain His appointed government, they honor Him who is the only King and Law-giver in Zion. And as thus the Church in her doctrines, worship, government and life exalts her Prophet, glorifies her Priest, and honors her King, the life of the God-man flows through her, and she becomes instinct with a new power and a glorious light, and is at once an Evangel to all nations, and a manifestation unto principalities and powers, in heavenly places, of the manifold wisdom of God.

CHAPTER IX.

The Spirituality of the Kingdom.

THE charge preferred by the Jews against Jesus before the tribunal of Pilate was, that He was Christ—a king—a rival of Cæsar, the Roman Emperor, whose agent and servant Pilate was. Jesus admitted the truth of the charge that He was a king; but denied that He was any rival of Cæsar. Nor was there any need of any conflict of claims or powers between Christ and Cæsar. The kingdom of Cæsar was of the world; the kingdom of Christ, so Jesus expressly declared, was not of this world; if it had been a worldly kingdom like Cæsar's, then His servants would have fought for Him.

Jesus had before this enunciated the same great principle, that there was no occasion for any collision between the Church and the State. Render unto Cæsar the things that are Cæsar's, and render unto God the things that are God's.

He distinctly recognizes the co-existence of two kingdoms—the kingdom of God and the kingdom of Cæsar; the Church of Christ and the Civil authority.

In point of time and thought the Family institution precedes both Church and State; and upon this institution, both Church and State rest as a natural basis; that is, both of them are composed, not of individual units, but of *families.*

The State is an ordinance of God; for the powers that be are ordained of God; the Civil Magistrate is God's agent, and he beareth not the sword in vain. It follows then, with absolute certainty, that every soul must be subject to the higher authorities; and that tribute must paid to those to whom the *tribute is due;* custom to whom the custom is due, fear to whom fear, honor to whom honor. *Cæsar must have all his dues*, for so Christ commanded. And IF allegiance BE DUE to Cæsar, then Cæsar must have it.

Some kind of organized government would have arisen and existed among men had the race never sinned against God. Civil Government is for man the *creature*, and is from God as *Creator*. The State, therefore, does not handle the Revealed Will of the King in Zion; nor does it deal with problems of sin and redemption. It legislates for the creature in the light of reason and the moral law, which is binding upon all creatures.

God delegated to the people the power to establish governments among men, but He prescribed no *form* through which the delegated power should be exercised; hence *any* form may be established—despotism, monarchy, republic, or democracy; hence, too, the right of the people to change, modify, or abrogate any form of government under which they live.

The subject-matter of State legislation is persons and property; the rights of the citizen, the protection of property; and this legislation is for time; it does not reach forward to eternity.

The end which the State is intended to accomplish is to enable the citizens to lead quiet and peaceable lives, in all godliness and honesty.

In order that the State may enforce its laws concerning persons and property, and secure to its citizens quiet and peaceable lives, it is armed with, and carries as its symbol, the sword.

Side by side with this temporal worldly kingdom of Cæsar there moves the spiritual, eternal kingdom of Christ, which, though *in* the world, is yet not *of* the world. The questions which, by the appointment of God, belong to the State do not belong in anywise to the Church; and the questions which, by the appointment of Christ, belong to the Church do not belong in anywise to the State.

The Church is a mediatorial kingdom—is founded upon and is derived from Jesus Christ as Mediator; it is a government ordained and organized for man the *sinner*, not for man the *creature;* had there been no sin, there had been no Church.

The light that was sufficient for man the creature is insufficient for man the sinner; hence the Mediator in founding his kingdom must give light, and that light is His revealed will, and this will, as contained in the Statute Book of the kingdom, is the only and all-sufficient rule of Church action. And as the whole matter of redemption for the sinner is a question of pure revelation, the form of the Messianic kingdom is appointed and revealed by Him who is Head and Lord of that kingdom. It exists under a written charter and constitution, and outside of this it dare not go.

The Church deals with souls, and reaches onward to the eternity before us all.

The end which the Church proposes to accomplish is the salvation of sinners, and therein the glory of God. It bears no sword, but the keys of the kingdom of heaven are given to it by

Him who built the kingdom. It has no right to wear the sword nor to inflict temporal penalties. It is obvious at a glance that Church and State differ most widely in their structure, powers and ends.

1. The State is from God; the Church is from the Mediator.

2. The State is for the Creature; the Church for the sinner.

3. The State bears the sword; the Church the keys.

4. The State secures peaceable lives; the Church the salvation of sinners.

5. The State deals with persons and property; the Church deals with souls.

If the State keeps within the limits assigned to it by God, and the Church keeps within the limits assigned it by the Mediator, it is impossible for any conflict ever to arise; and, in fact, no conflict ever arises until one or the other transcends its proper province, and undertakes to settle matters over which it has no jurisdiction.

In reference to those mixed questions which are partly civil and partly ecclesiastical, the principles above indicated prevail. The State handles the civil, and the Church takes charge of the spiritual interests of the mixed question. Slavery, the observance of the Sabbath, the marriage relation—these and various other questions have a twofold aspect, but in every case the State determines the civil part of the problem in the light of nature, reason, history, and the moral law; the Church settles the religious part of the problem solely in the light of revelation.

But, says some one, may not the Church testify against *all sin?* is not the Church a witness for the King of Heaven? and must she not lift up her voice against all transgressions of the Divine Law? Must not the Church declare against the sin of slavery, treason and rebellion? *Certainly it is the right and the solemn duty of the Church to testify against all sin.* If she will be a faithful witness for Jesus, she *must* do this.

But in bearing this testimony, the Church must never go beyond or *aside* from the Word of her King in defining what sin is. If Christ either expressly or by fair inference says that slaveholding is sinful, the Church is bound to declare that the slaveholder is an offender against God; but if Christ has never pronounced slavery sinful, then the Church dare not condemn the slaveholder as a transgressor of the Divine Law. There is no other rule for the Church than the King's Revealed Will. So far as the question of treason and rebellion is concerned, the King in Zion has never defined either term. The Church cannot punish treason or rebellion, because it has no authoritative information from the Word of God as to what constitutes either treason or rebellion.

Crime cannot be punished unless the crime be defined: the statute books of the State may define treason and rebellion; but the Statute Book of the heavenly kingdom does not define either. The State, then, may punish traitors and rebels; the Church cannot punish either.

The moment the Church defines rebellion and issues process or anathema against the rebel, she has passed *outside* of her sphere and province, and has become an interpreter and judge of civil law, which belongs exclusively to the State.

The Church has no right to interpret civil law, for God gave her no such commission; she is a witness for Christ, to declare the things written in the Book, and since the Book is silent upon all these questions of allegiance, loyalty, treason and rebellion, the Church dare not open her mouth.

But does not the Book command us to be subject to the powers that be? to render to Cæsar the things that are Cæsar's? to pay tribute to whom tribute is due, and custom to whom custom? Certainly, the Word of God does so com-

The Spirituality of the Kingdom.

mand, and the Church must so teach; but the same word does not define *who* are the higher powers, nor does it tell or give us any criteria by which we can determine *who* is our Cæsar; nor does it declare to *whom* the tribute is due: it leaves the citizen to determine for himself, and takes for granted that he has settled the question, who is Cæsar, and to whom the tribute is due; and then it commands the citizen to pay the tribute, and to render to Cæsar the things that are his.

The mistake the Church has so frequently made was, that it did *not stop* where the command of God *ceased;* it went beyond the Written Law of the Spiritual kingdom; and determined authoritatively, and in the name of God, who was the citizen's Cæsar, and to whom the tribute was due. And as these were questions not settled in the Statute Book of the mediatorial kingdom, of course the Church had no shadow of right to utter any opinions whatever concerning them.

If the Bible defined treason or rebellion as it defines murder or theft or adultery, then the Church would be bound to treat treason or rebellion just as she treats murder or adultery. But the very fact that theft, murder, and other crimes are defined in the Word of God, while treason and rebellion are left undefined, is a proof that Jesus Christ has left the latter to the State for definition and punishment.

The guilt or innocence of the citizen, as a member of the civil organization, is to be determined entirely by the laws of the Commonwealth under which he lives; as these laws are interpreted one way, he is guilty; as interpreted in a different way, he is innocent. It is impossible in the very nature of the case for any ecclesiastical tribunal, sitting in the name and acting by the authority and guided by the Written Word of Jesus Christ, to form or to express any opinion as to the proper interpretation of the laws of the land: the name, authority, and Word of the King are all silent, and how dare the Church speak in His name and by His authority when He never gave her any authority, and when He Himself has never spoken? To suppose that such testimony of the Church is in accordance with the commission to preach Christ and Him crucified, is a stretch of the law ecclesiastical reserved to the modern lights of latter days in Church and State.

The kingdom not of this world must not handle the constitutions and laws that are of this world. As the Church may not handle civil matters that pertain to the Commonwealth, so the State is not a teacher of religion nor a judge of the things revealed in the Statute Book of the Messianic kingdom. In so far as members of the Church are also citizens of the State, they are protected in their persons and property; and when it is necessary for the Church in its organic capacity to have recourse to law, the State provides for the appointment of certain persons who shall act as trustees for the Church. The most of the United States do not recognize the existence of the Church, as such, but deal with it only through trustees.

It is a right of the State, whenever the Church becomes an injury to the Commonwealth, to prohibit, by proper legislation, any injury that may arise to its citizens; but if the State forbids the Church to do what Christ commanded, or commands what Christ forbids, then the Church must obey God rather than men. If the Church will keep within her proper sphere, she has little to apprehend from unfriendly State legislation.

The very fact that the Church is founded upon the Mediator of the Covenant of Redemption lies at the basis of her Spirituality. The King in Zion is no earthly, temporal King; He is an invisible, eternal, heavenly prince. Having shed His blood to redeem His Church, He has ascended up into heaven, is seated upon His mediatorial throne, and from thence, by His Spirit and

Word, He rules as King in Zion. His throne is in the heavens.

The spirituality of the kingdom is further evident from the fact that the Holy Spirit is Vicar of Christ, and is at work in the hearts of Christ's subjects, working in them to will and to do the King's good pleasure. There is no force, no coercion in this reign of Christ; all is love—love to an unseen Saviour—for the love of Christ constraineth us.

The members of this kingdom are spiritual; the holy, the regenerated, the saints, the spiritually-minded; they who walk not after the flesh, but after the Spirit, and who are led by the Spirit.

The mission of this kingdom is purely spiritual. Its great commission is, Preach the Gospel, make disciples, baptize them in the name of the Holy Three; train them for eternity. It teaches men revealed truth unto salvation; it worships God in the Spirit. Its great work is to make known the will of the King as contained in His Holy Word; with questions aside from this Word it has nothing whatever to do. The sanctions, too, by which the Church enforces its authority are also spiritual. The Church carries no sword, but the keys of the kingdom. It declares the King's will, administers the King's government, and opens and shuts the doors of the Spiritual House. The weapons of the Church's warfare are not carnal, but spiritual, and are mighty through the power of God to the accomplishment of all spiritual ends.

Different in its structure from all earthly kingdoms, with a revealed Doctrine, a prescribed Worship, and a Divinely-appointed Government; distinct and separate from the State by the decree of Christ, and by His Work as Builder; derived from and founded upon the Mediator, with an invisible spiritual King, who rules over the kingdom after a spiritual manner; composed of the spiritually-minded, whom it trains for eternity unto God's glory; with a spiritual doctrine to proclaim, and with nothing wherewith to enforce its authority except spiritual sanction, we need not hesitate to reaffirm the declaration of the King, that His kingdom is not of this world.

CHAPTER X.

The Unity of the Church.

THE idea of unity was never more fully realized than in the history of the Jewish nation. God segregated them from the other nations of the earth, and by the most rigid enactments prevented them from mixing with other people. The uncircumcised Gentile was an object of scorn to the descendant of the father of the faithful.

But when the Son of God died upon the cross, this middle wall of partition was broken down, and the uncircumcised Gentiles were admitted to all the privileges of the Christian Church upon the very same terms as the Jews were admitted.

In Christ Jesus all distinctions according to the flesh are completely and for ever abolished. In Him there is neither Jew nor Greek; there is neither bond nor free; there is neither male nor female, for ye are all one in Christ.

The Incarnation of the Son of God, the

assumption of our *common humanity*, seals for ever the brotherhood of man. God hath made of one blood all the nations of the earth, and in his Incarnate Son all men are brothers.

The Christian Church rests upon the Incarnation and Headship of Jesus Christ as the Divine basis, and the universal brotherhood of man as the human basis of its unity.

When once a man has entered into the kingdom of Jesus Christ, then no matter whether he be Jew or Gentile, Scythian or Barbarian, bond or free, Greek or Roman, Caucasian or negro, he is one with Christ, and one with all those who are in Christ. He has every right and every privilege in the Church that any other member has—right to the Word and the Sacraments; the right to vote in all Church elections, and to be voted for. We say a *man*, for *women* are prohibited by the written command of the King from holding certain offices; but any man who has the proper qualifications may be called by the Lord Jesus to hold any office in His kingdom; and if the call to the man from the Head of the Church be clear, then the Church dare not withhold ordination. To deny any member of the kingdom of heaven any right or privilege of his brother members is to strike at the unity of the Church itself. If the King has made any restrictive regulations in His kingdom, of course the Church is bound to obey those regulations. The great principle is, however, clear and indisputable, that in Christ all distinctions of race, color and caste cease for ever—all are one in Him.

This principle must be limited by the statement that Christ was no agrarian, and the Church is no society of communists, nor is the Church intended to break down the framework of society, and to teach the Jacobin doctrine of liberty, equality and fraternity. Let every man abide in the same calling wherein he was called, is also a law of the universal kingdom.

In one of the last recorded conversations of the Divine Man He prays most earnestly for the unity of His people, that they all may be one, even as He and the Father were one, and He declares that there is one fold and one Shepherd.

Jesus Christ represents Himself as the Head, and the Church as His body; and though there are many members in the body, yet, as there is one Head, so also there is but one Body. And this body of Christ, is pervaded by one common life—the life of the Holy Spirit, the Comforter; and this Headship of Christ, and this life from the Spirit constitute the organic Unity of the Church.

This organic Unity does not depend upon any one visible Head, as the Pope, or a College of Bishops, as the successor of the Apostolic College, but it depends upon an Invisible Head, the risen and enthroned Redeemer, and the pulsations of a common life, derived from the Holy Ghost.

There are many branches, yet but one Vine; there are many stones, yet but one Temple; there are many children and brethren, yet but one family in heaven and on earth; there are many mansions, yet but one house and one home for all the saints. There is one Lord, one Faith, one Baptism, one God and Father of all, who is above all, and through all, and in you all; and the Saviour's last prayer for all who believe is, that they may be one, as Thou Father art in Me, and I in Thee, that they also may be one in Us.

Starting with this view of the Unity of Christ's kingdom as given by Himself, when we look at the Christian Church of the present day we see on all sides divisions and diversities. The ideal unity of the Church as presented in the Word of God does not seem to be realized in the outward life of the Church.

In the same local church organization, there are diversities of gifts; to one, is given the word of wisdom; to another, faith; to another, the gift of healing; to another, prophecy; to another, charity.

Again, even in churches of the same faith and order, as they are called, all the churches under one supreme supervision are not united in the same local organization; but there are particular churches in different localities.

Add to this, that Church organizations generally follow State and national boundaries; hence we have the Church of England, the Church of Ireland, and the various non-State Churches of the different countries of the globe.

And still further, there are different denominations or sects of Christians, having separate ecclesiastical organizations, throughout nearly all the Christianized parts of the world.

When we pursue this line of inquiry, we find different creeds, different hymn-books, different forms of worship and government; so that we are ready to despair of finding any unity in these different and diverse organizations.

But if the Mystical Body of Christ be one, then the outward manifestation of that body, the visibility of the Church, must also give evidence of unity—the shadow must present the outlines of the substance that casts the shadow.

It is evident, that uniformity does not constitute unity—organic, vital unity. There is perfect uniformity in the walls of a marble palace; each block of marble may be of the same size, and present the very same appearance as his fellow; and yet though this be the case, and the entire walls of the palace be uniform, there is no unity, for each block is separate and distinct from every other block; and the whole mass is held together, not by any organic life or principle of unity, but entirely by artificial means.

The oak of the forest gives the idea of unity, in contrast with the uniformity of the wall; each leaf, and branch, and root, and fibre is different from every other; yet there is an organic life flowing from lowest root to topmost leaf, and the whole tree produces upon the mind of the beholder the idea of unity.

The Papal conception of the unity of the Church is no unity at all, but the dull uniformity of one of the marble palaces of the Pope.

Unity does not anywhere consist in *uniformity*, but the highest possible *unity* is manifested and developed in the midst of *diversities*.

Mind and matter, two totally different things, united in the person of a human being, give one of the highest forms of unity, man. He is one, though composed of elements so unlike and diverse.

The most perfect of all unities, the unity of the Divine Being, manifests itself in diversity. The essence of the Godhead is one; yet this one essence manifests itself to men in three distinct and separate Persons—the Father, Son, and Holy Ghost; and yet there is but one God.

In the human body there are many members; hands, eyes, feet, arms, and limbs, and yet the body is one—its unity exists in the midst of diversity: so with the Body of Christ, there are many members, many denominations, many diversities, and yet but one Church of the Living God. And just as every member of the human body has its place and use, so all these different Churches and denominations have their place and use in the Body of Christ.

And when we come to a closer examination of these differences among Christians and Churches, we shall find them more apparent than real: in all the essential elements of the life of the Church there is remarkable concord and unity.

There are three great departments which embrace the sum total of the outward life and activities of the Church; and if the ideal unity of the Church, as taught in the Scriptures, can be manifested in the life of the Church, it must be in these departments; and if in these particulars that unity is seen, then the *visible* unity of of the God-man's kingdom is no less certain than its invisible unity.

The total activities of the outward life of the

Church may be thus classified, viz.: Doctrine, Worship, and Government. When the Doctrine or Faith of the Church is given, together with the object and mode of its Worship, and the Government, it seems that there is no activity of the Church that will not fall into one or the other of these departments.

As the structure of the kingdom consisted of a Revealed Doctrine, a Prescribed Worship, and an Ordained Government, as the marks of the true Church are to be found in its Doctrine, Worship and Government, so also the outward unity of the Church is seen in these three grand elements.

Now it may be safely asserted that in these three departments of the outward life of the Church there is substantial agreement:

1. Unity of Doctrine.

In reference to the Supreme Being, the object of all religion, there are no discordant notes given forth by any creed or confession of any true Church of Jesus Christ. Hear, O Israel! the Lord our God is One Lord.

The starting-point of all evangelical doctrine of all Christians on the face of the earth is the absolute and perfect unity of the Deity.

But in this one essence, so the common faith of the Church of God teaches, there are three Divine Persons—Father, Son, and Holy Ghost—

of the same substance, equal in power and glory.

The Spirituality of God is also a fundamental article in the creed of the Church; and they who worship God must worship Him in Spirit and in truth.

The creed called by the name of the Apostles, though not composed by them, believed by all Christians and all Churches, taught in the Sabbath-schools, recited in the congregations of believers, accepted throughout all Christendom as a brief summary of the common faith, thus declares the doctrine concerning the Deity: I believe in God the Father Almighty, Maker of Heaven and Earth; in Jesus Christ His only Son, our Lord; I believe in the Holy Ghost, the Holy Catholic Church, the Communion of Saints, the Forgiveness of Sins, the Resurrection of the Body, and the Life Everlasting.

If we pass now to consider the doctrine concerning the person and work of the Mediator, Him who stands as the middle term between God and man, here, too, there is substantial unity among all bodies of Christians. All recognize Him as God, manifest in the flesh; as both human and Divine, in one Person, the Person of the Son of God: this Divine man, thus wonderfully constituted, renders a perfect obedience to the precept of the law, and endures its full and fearful penalty, and thus becomes to all those who believe in Him the end of the law for righteousness. He is a Saviour able and willing to save unto the uttermost all who will come unto Him. I believe, says the creed of the whole Church, in Jesus Christ, the Only-Begotten Son, our Lord, who was conceived by the Holy Ghost, born of the Virgin, suffered under Pontius Pilate, was crucified, dead and buried; the third day He rose again from the dead, He ascended into heaven, and sitteth on the right hand of God, the Father Almighty, from thence He shall come to judge the quick and the dead.

The God-man is the one great theme of all Revelation; the central figure of the common salvation; the object of the faith of the Church of God under every Dispensation of the covenant of Redemption. "He is the Lord whose future coming cheered the saintly Enoch; the Redeemer on whom Job rested his hopes of immortality, when in the latter days he should stand upon the earth; the Seed of Abraham in whom all nations were to be blest; the Shiloh of Jacob's dying bed; the Angel of the covenant at the Burning Bush and in the cloudy fiery pillar; the Captain who fought for Israel's hosts and nerved the hearts of Israel's warriors;

the Virgin-born Immanuel foretold by Isaiah when he saw His glory, and spake of Him as the Wonderful Counsellor; the Messiah announced by Daniel, cut off not for Himself but for His people; the Fourth Form in the fiery furnace, walking with the Hebrew children; the Fountain opened in the House of David for sin and uncleanness;" the Infant whom Simeon blest; the Jesus whom the Angel named; the dying Saviour in whom the penitent Thief trusted; the Son of God on the cross whom the Centurion acknowledged; the risen Rabboni whom Mary adored; and the Infinitely Precious Redeemer of all God's saints in all ages, and of every kindred and tongue and tribe and people.

Passing now to consider *Man* the subject of religion, here, too, the testimony of all creeds and confessions is to the effect, that man is a guilty, depraved, miserable being, and that unless saved from sin by the grace of God, he must perish for evermore. It is true there are differences upon the *non-essential* points, of how man came into this estate of sin and misery, and the precise extent of His connection with Adam in his first disobedience, but these are matters *not* vital to his salvation: the great fact that man is a sinner is accepted by all who are part of the true Church.

So also with reference to other precious doctrines of Revelation,—that the Bible is a perfect rule of faith and practice; that there is a future State of rewards for the righteous, and punishments for the wicked; that there is to be a Resurrection of the dead, and a general Judgment — upon these doctrines the faith of the Church is emphatically *one*.

The statements just made as regards the unity of the Church in the matter of doctrine may be verified by consulting the symbols of all the Reformed Churches on the continent of Europe; the Confessions of the Scotch, Irish, Welsh, and Moravian Churches, the Articles of the Church of England, the Catechism of the Lutheran and German Reformed Churches, the Books of Discipline of the Methodist Churches, the Standards of the Presbyterian and Baptist Churches, and in short, all the symbolic books of all bodies recognized as parts of the visible kingdom of the Divine man.

2. The unity of the Church is no less visible in the matter of Worship than in the department of Doctrine.

There are three particulars that are decisive of the question of unity of worship: they are, the object of worship; the sincerity of the worshiper; and the worship rendered, to be regulated in the manner prescribed by the object of the worship. Where there is agreement in these three particulars there is unity of worship.

Now as to the *object* of religious worship, all Protestant Churches hold most tenaciously that the only proper object of worship is the Infinite God—Father, Son, and Holy Ghost. Thou shalt worship the Lord thy God, and Him only shalt thou serve. Worship offered to any other object is not religious worship, but *idolatry*.

Nor is there any difference of sentiment as to the sincerity of the worshiper. God is a Spirit, and they who worship Him must worship Him in spirit and in truth.

So also with regard to the several acts and parts of worship; it is conceded by all Churches, that these acts and parts of worship must be those prescribed by the King in His revealed Word.

When one enters the different Churches, he finds great apparent diversity in the worship offered to the Most High. In some assemblies, the worshipers stand while they sing; in others, they stand and pray, and sit while they sing—some kneel at the Lord's Supper, and others sit while they receive the sacred memorials. Some ministers pray extempore, and others read from the prayer-book. But a closer inspection shows that these are mere differences of posture, while the essential parts of worship are the same in all the Churches.

First and foremost, in all assemblies of the King's true worshipers, you will find the Word of God, the Scriptures of the Old and New Testament, the Infallible Rule of Belief and Duty. This Revealed Will of the King, this Statute Book of the kingdom, holds the prominent place in all true Churches of Jesus Christ. Sabbath after Sabbath, wide over all the earth, in all the assemblies of the Saints, this Book is read in the hearing of the people, and expounded unto them.

Again, prayer and praise are parts of worship prescribed by the King in Zion; and into whatever house of God a man may enter, whether Established or Dissenter, whether Lutheran or Reformed, whether Baptist, Methodist, or Presbyterian, he will hear the voice of thanksgiving, intercession, and supplication going up to the God that heareth and answereth prayer. And if a worshiping assembly be found where no voice of prayer is heard, it may be safely assumed Jesus Christ does not claim it as any part of His heritage.

The God-man has appointed that His people shall worship Him in the singing of Psalms and Hymns and Spiritual Songs; and in nothing is the unity of the Church more palpably seen than in its Hymnology. The Psalms of David form a part of almost every collection of sacred music that is used in the praise of the Almighty; while the great majority of hymns used in the service of the Sanctuary are found in all the Hymn-books of the different branches of the true Church. Such, for example, as—

"Rock of Ages! cleft for me"—"Alas, and did my Saviour bleed?"—"There is a Fountain filled with blood!"—"Amazing grace! how sweet the sound!"—"Jesus, lover of my soul!"—these and scores of others are known and loved and sung by all who are called by the name of Christ.

Sacraments and Almsgiving complete the list of prescribed acts of Worship.

The true Church of Jesus Christ has never recognized but *two* Sacraments as appointed by the Head of the Church; and these are Baptism and the Lord's Supper. There are differences among true Christians as to the subjects and mode of Baptism; but in the following essential elements there is no difference of opinion, viz.: Jesus Christ, as Founder and Head of the Church instituted the ordinance; it consists of the application of water to a person scripturally qualified to receive it; it is to be applied in the name of the Trinity, by a person authorized by Christ to administer the ordinance; and it signifies and seals to the worthy recipient the blessings of the New Covenant; and these particulars, wherein all agree, are the essence of the Sacrament.

Concerning the Lord's Supper, the sentiment of the Church is so completely a unit that nothing need be said in this connection.

The giving of alms on the Sabbath-day, and in the house of God, has been a part of the prescribed worship of the King's house from the days of the Patriarchs to the present time.

3. Unity of Government.

In this particular, it is frankly admitted there are more differences among the various denominations of Christians than in either the department of Doctrine or Worship; and yet a rigid analysis of the Government of the kingdom will show, that even here, in the midst of diversities, there is substantial unity.

Waiving any inquiry into the *four* forms of Church Government—the Papal, Prelatical, Presbyterian and Independent—and passing at once to consider the office-bearers and rule that are of the essence of the Government of the kingdom, we see at once, in all of our Churches, a certain class of men whose duty it is to proclaim the Finished Doctrine and to order the Worship of the Church. Call these men by any name, Bishop, Elder, Doctor, Teacher or Deacon, still here is the work for them to do, and that work is the same in all Churches, viz.: to preach the Word and to administer the ordinances of the kingdom.

So also there is a work of *ruling* in all Churches; and for this there is a class of Rulers, whose duty and work it is to take heed unto the Flock over which the Holy Ghost has made them Overseers. Here, again, the mere name is of no consequence; and the grant of more or less power to certain ones of these Rulers ought not to be esteemed a matter of vital moment.

But Doctrine, Discipline, and Distribution exhaust the list of office-bearers in the Spiritual kingdom; and if we find in all of our Churches certain persons who act as Distributors of the revenues of the King's treasury, then we have obtained the object of our search, viz.: unity of Church Government. There is a class of office-bearers, in all branches of the true Church, who attend upon this very matter. Some call these men Stewards; others, Deacons; others, Vestrymen; the name is nothing, the reality only concerns us.

If the foregoing analysis be correct, then the unity of the Visible Church is established; for if Doctrine, Worship, and Government cover the totality of the outward life of the Church, and if there is substantial agreement in these particulars among the various sects, then the outward unity of the Spiritual kingdom is proved.

There is a very popular and prevalent idea now-a-days that there is no unity of the Church of Christ so long as there are different Church organizations and denominations; and there is a great, pious, canting cry for the breaking down of all denominational barriers, and the herding of all the sheep in one great Union Commons — that each branch of the true Church must give up some of its distinctive features, and all the various sects must form a Church Union. The *advanced thought* cries aloud for *co-operative Christianity*. The body of Christ must be taken to pieces: hands, eyes, feet, arms, must all be plucked out and cut off, and the disjoined members put into the great Union Cauldron and made over into a New Union Church; and the Churchman who enters not into these pious schemes is called a bigot. This is nothing but a re-hash of the old Papal theory of Church unity; it is the uniformity of the wall, not the living unity of the tree, the unity of the Gospel. The highest types of unity are, as we have seen, perfectly compatible with the greatest diversities; and the unity of the Visible Church is perfectly compatible with the most vigorous denominational life.

The tribes of Israel, when they took the line of march for the Promised Land, did not go in one union mob, but each tribe under its own flag and its own leader; so let the chosen tribes of the Spiritual Israel, who are journeying to the Better Land, march each tribe under its own chosen leaders and with its own distinctive banner; for high over all the tribes and all the banners is the banner stained with blood, and the Captain who leads the whole host is the Incarnate Son of God; and to all the tribes the same heavenly manna is given, and the same cloudy fiery pillar guides them all. Give us, then, a vigorous denominational life and love; and while there is such remarkable unity of Doctrine, Worship, and Government, let not the tribes fall out by the way, but present a united front to the common enemy of them all.

The unity of the Spiritual kingdom will not be fully realized and manifested in time; but the Head of the kingdom assures us that the day will come when all the scattered sheep of the Fold shall be gathered together in one fold and under one Shepherd; when the teachings of Scripture and the longings of the Saints shall be alike realized; when the scaffoldings that now hide the beauty and unity of the living and

Spiritual Temple shall all be taken down; and when the New Jerusalem, the Bride of the Lamb, all prepared and adorned for her husband, shall descend from God out of heaven to possess the New Heavens and the New Earth.

CHAPTER XI.

Baptism, the Law of Membership.

IT is a matter of the utmost importance to understand and to state the terms upon which any one may become a citizen of this Spiritual kingdom; and it is gratifying to know that the King himself has laid down the invariable law of admission into His kingdom.

The man to whom Jesus stated the mode and law of admission was surprised at the words of the King. How can a man be born when he is old? can he enter the second time into his mother's womb and be born?—was his inquiry to the statement that the New Birth was the mode and law of admission into the kingdom of heaven. Nicodemus confined his ideas to the material and temporal. He did not comprehend that the kingdom of heaven had no earthly origin, no earthly Head; that it was governed by no earthly constitution, administered by no earthly laws; was neither advanced nor retarded by earthly power. He did not realize that the kingdom into which He sought admission had a Divine Head, a Heavenly origin, and was governed by Spiritual influences. Like its glorious Author, it cometh not with observation: and while one is looking here and another there for the King and His kingdom, the testimony of Christ is, that His kingdom is within the soul.

The kingdom is Spiritual and supernatural; hence it follows, of necessity, that the mode of admission, the law of membership must be Spiritual and supernatural. We ought not therefore to be surprised, as Nicodemus was, when the King proclaims the law: *Verily, verily, I say unto thee, except a man be born again, he cannot see the kingdom of God.* So, then, no man can become a citizen of the heavenly kingdom except by the New Birth of the soul. This New Birth is the work of the Spirit of the God, for so the Divine Teacher expressly declared to the Jewish Ruler. Except a man be born of water, and *of the Spirit*, he cannot enter into the kingdom of God. *How* the Spirit causes the spiritual New Birth, the Regeneration of the soul, we know not—the work is spiritual, supernatural, invisible: even the wind bloweth where it listeth; we hear the sound, we see the effects, we know that the wind has been in motion; but how and whence it came, and whither it goeth, we know not: even so with those who are born of the Spirit; and if we understand not the mode of physical things, we need not expect to comprehend the *rationale* of heavenly things.

This work of the Spirit in the soul is a *new creation* in Christ Jesus, a Resurrection from spiritual death. It is the workmanship of God, independent of human instrumentalities: a birth, not of blood, nor of the will of the flesh, nor of the will of man, but a Divinely-begotten principle, of which the Holy Ghost is the Author.

It is not a joint work of God and man—the soul is passive, it is acted upon, and the Holy Spirit is the sole actor. It is the heart of stone that is made a heart of flesh. As the inanimate body of Adam lived not until Jehovah breathed into it the breath of life, so the dead soul lives not until the Holy Spirit implants the principle of Spiritual life. Regeneration is an act above the operations of nature, by which a tree that had been bringing forth evil fruit, now brings forth good fruit; by which a fountain that had been sending forth bitter water, now sends forth sweet water. It is a Birth, a Creation, a Resurrection.

The soul that is admitted into the Spiritual

kingdom is born of the Spirit, and is led to desire and to seek after Spiritual things. Quickened by the Spirit and risen with Christ, it seeks those things which are above: it looks not for an earthly Canaan, but for a city which hath foundations whose Maker and Builder is God.

This real, supernatural, spiritual change wrought in man by the Holy Ghost must not be confounded with a Reformation of manners and morals, however thorough such a Reformation may be. Regeneration is indeed Reformation; but Reformation is not Regeneration.

There are many sins the indulgence in which involves the loss of reputation, health, and property; and many a man has been induced to give up his sins and reform his life because he saw that his sins would ruin him: he gave up one temporal pleasure for a greater temporal good. But the new principle of life leads a man to give up all sins, and suffer the loss of all temporal good, if needs be, for the love he has for Christ.

The change wrought in the heart of man is not the mere change whereby the rogue determines to be an honest man—the liar, a speaker of the truth—or the lewd man, chaste: it is not a conflict against inveterate habits and bad society and evil example, wherein the man triumphs, and by great effort forces himself back into the ranks of good citizens and honest men; but it is a cleansing of the fountain of the heart, whence all the life of man flows—it is the purifying of the source of the stream—it is a new principle of life; old things pass away—all things are made new.

Nor is Regeneration to be confounded with the most blameless life of outward morality. A man may be a pattern of all external morality; he may keep all the commandments from his youth up, as the young Jew did; and still he is not a member of the Spiritual kingdom, unless he has experienced *within* the supernatural change. What is absolutely necessary is not *morality*, but *life;* ye must be born again.

Nor can this new principle of Spiritual life be produced by any change in the governing purpose of the will; for the sons of God, the members of the Spiritual kingdom, are not born of the will of the flesh, nor of the will of man.

As we see daily in the lives of our fellow-men, the most powerful motives that can be addressed to the will fail to lead the sinner to love holiness for its own sake, and to follow Christ in the regeneration. A will that is corrupt and depraved will never choose holiness in preference to sin; and as the nature that lies back of the will, and controls all of its motions, is also depraved, the case is utterly hopeless, so far as man is concerned; ye must be born of water and of the *Spirit*.

This New Birth is Baptism, the Baptism of the Holy Ghost, the only Baptism that Jesus Christ ever administered; it is the inward law of membership in His kingdom—His mark in the foreheads of His Elect. Verily, I say unto thee, Except a man be *born again*, except he be Baptized with the Holy Ghost, he cannot see the kingdom of God.

But the Spiritual kingdom of the Divine Man is also a Visible kingdom among men; the subjects of this kingdom are men in the flesh, brought together into the Christian Church, which is constituted and made visible by certain divinely-appointed ordinances, viz.: Doctrine, Worship, and Government.

The mode of admission into the Visible Church must correspond with the mode of admission into the invisible Spiritual kingdom: as men enter the invisible kingdom, by the Baptism of the Holy Ghost, so the King hath appointed an outward ordinance of water Baptism to symbolize the Baptism of the Spirit.

Water Baptism is not a *charm*, possessing some secret, indefinable power to cure the leprosy of sin, or to drive away moral or physical evil, or prevent the commission or punishment of sin.

Nor is water Baptism a *grace-working* Sacrament, conveying Spiritual blessings in virtue of its own inherent efficacy and power: thousands have received water Baptism, and have lived and died without experiencing the saving grace of God. All the water under the heavens cannot remove one sin from the soul.

Nor is it a mere *arbitrary* ordinance. True, it is appointed by the Sovereign of the Spiritual kingdom, appointed in virtue of His kingly authority; but there is nothing *arbitrary* about it: so far as we can see, it could not have been anything else. The resemblance, correspondence, connection between the Baptism of the Spirit and the Baptism with water is close and complete. The appointment of the King is founded upon this relation between the two Baptisms. And the whole significance of water Baptism lies in the fact that it symbolizes the Baptism of the Holy Ghost.

There is the outward sign—the water; the inward grace signified—regeneration; and the correspondence and sacramental union between the sign and the thing signified; and to all worthy recipients of Baptism it is a *seal* as well as a sign.

In the Baptism of the Spirit man *receives* a

divine, quickening, and purifying influence; in the water Baptism man must also *receive* the water, in token of the Spirit's work. He is never *put into* the Holy Ghost; so he ought never to be *put into* and *under* the water. In both cases the subject is *acted upon from above*.

It was prophesied that Messiah should *sprinkle* many nations; the word was fulfilled upon the day of Pentecost, when many nations were representatively gathered at Jerusalem, and the ascended King *shed down upon them* the Holy Ghost, and the Apostles *sprinkled* three thousand with water.

The invariable practice of the Apostles was to *apply* the *water* to the subject; they never *applied* the *subject* to the water.

When Cornelius and his friends were gathered in his house to hear the words of Peter, as Peter spake the Holy Ghost *fell upon* them; then Peter remembered his Master's words concerning the Spirit's Baptism, and he called for water, and there in the *house*, the *room* where they were assembled, he *applied* the water to those upon whom the Spirit fell.

So when Ananias baptized Saul of Tarsus, he did not say, Arise, let us go to the river Pharpar; but *stand upon thy feet*, and here in the *house* where you now are, *receive* the water Baptism, in token of your Spiritual cleansing.

Nor is there any account of preparation made for the Baptism of the jailor at Philippi; no changes of raiment, no Baptisteries, no bath-houses; but in the *same hour* of his believing he brought them from the *inner* prison to the part of the same building occupied by his family, and washed the stripes of Paul and Silas, and was *straightway* baptized by them.

And in all these cases the word of Jehovah was fulfilled: Then will I SPRINKLE clean water upon you; I will *pour* my Spirit upon thy seed; then shall He *sprinkle* many nations. To dip, or plunge, or immerse, or submerge the body of the believer into the liquid grave is to destroy the whole significance of the ordinance and the entire resemblance between the sign and the thing signified. And to connect water Baptism with the *burial* of Christ's body is wholly to misunderstand the phrase Buried with Him in Baptism, for this alludes in nowise to His body, but to His *Baptism of Suffering* in Gethsemane and at Calvary.

Baptism is, also, to the proper subject, a seal of the saving grace of the Spirit, and of the blessings secured to the Elect in the Covenant of Redemption. Baptism is a *Covenant* ordinance, and as such it is, to the proper subject, the Seal, the Pledge of the Mediator and Executor of that Covenant that He will faithfully perform all of His engagements to and for His people. Where the subject is a proper one, Regeneration is always signified and *sealed* by Baptism; for the sign and seal are not man's, but God's, and appointed by the Lord Jesus, according to the provisions of a Covenant, the conditions of which have all been fulfilled.

But Baptism and Regeneration, the sign and the thing signified, are not always indissolubly connected together. Sometimes Regeneration may precede Baptism by many years; Abraham believed long before he received the sign of the Covenant. Sometimes Baptism may precede Regeneration by many years, as is the case in scores and hundreds of instances.

It is a mistake to suppose that an unregenerate person can have no ecclesiastical right to water Baptism. The King himself declares that the tares will grow with the wheat; that the foolish virgins will go forth with the wise to meet the Bridegroom; and that bad as well as good fishes will be taken in the Gospel net. A perfectly pure Church is the hope of a better dispensation; it will never be realized in the present one.

As the Church has not power to read the

heart, so she may admit to her communion those who profess to have been born again, but who have never felt the renewing power of the Holy Spirit; such persons, when they make a satisfactory profession of conversion, are entitled to and should receive Baptism, as did Simon Magus, though he was in the gall of bitterness and the bonds of iniquity.

Who are the proper subjects of Baptism in the sight of God is one thing: who are entitled to ecclesiastical Baptism is a different thing.

Who are entitled to Baptism is a question to be decided wholly by what the King has said: as the kingdom is His, He only has the right to say who shall be entitled to receive its signs and seals.

There can be no doubt that all those who make satisfactory professions of their faith are entitled to Baptism; but there has been doubt expressed by some as to whether the children of Church members were entitled to the same ordinance.

Baptism is a Covenant ordinance, and belongs to the Spiritual kingdom, made visible among men. Now it is a universal law of all kingdoms that children take the status of their parents: a child born in Scotland is a Scotch child, and in virtue of his birth-right is entitled to the privileges and protection of Scotch law;

and when he arrives at legal age he has all the rights of a citizen. A child born in one of the United States is a member of that particular State wherein he was born, and is protected by that State: so the child born in the Visible kingdom of the God-man is a member of that kingdom, and is entitled to the privileges and blessings of that kingdom. Christ's kingdom is not so unlike all other kingdoms that the moment a child is born into it, he is cast out of it, over into the kingdom of darkness, to be the child of the Devil. Lambs born of a man's flock receive the owner's mark, not to make them his, but because they are his: so the little ones of the Good Shepherd's flock receive his mark, Baptism, because they are his, and Baptism is their covenanted birth-right.

The Church exists under the Covenant made with Abraham, and made with him as a Church member: if this Covenant has been abrogated, then the Church as a visible society has no charter, nor does it stand in any covenanted relations towards its Head and King.

If any adult in the present day is entitled to Baptism, it is because he professes the same faith which Abraham had, being yet uncircumcised: they that are of faith are blessed with faithful Abraham; but Abraham's *houschold* received the sign of the Covenant: so the *housc-*

holds of believers now ought to receive the sign of the same Covenant, for they that are Christ's are Abraham's seed, and heirs of the *same* promise. It is true the outward sign of circumcision has passed over into Baptism, but the Covenant, which is the all-important thing, remains ever the same; for there is no law of the King that has changed the Constitution of the Church as given to faithful Abraham.

So far from the children of Church members being driven out of the kingdom of Christ and their fathers, Peter expressly declared to the Jews, after the Spirit had been poured out and the Christian dispensation was fully inaugurated, Ye are still living under the Covenant made with Abraham, and the promise now, as then, is not only to you, but to your *children* also.

The promise, I will be a God to thee and thy seed has come upon the Gentiles through faith; and it is as great an offence now to deny the sign and seal of the Covenant to the children of Church members as it was in the days of Abraham and Moses.

And, says the Apostle Paul, one parent being a Church member settles the status of the children; for if the believing wife does not sanctify the unbelieving husband, then were your children unclean, but now are they holy; *i. e.*, federally holy, and entitled to Baptism, the sign and seal of the Covenant.

And in accordance with these plain provisions of the Charter and the Covenant of the Church, we read of whole *houscholds* being baptized upon the faith of one or both parents. The *household* of Stephanas was baptized by an inspired Apostle: so were the *households* of Lydia and the jailor at Philippi; and Peter baptized the *household* of Cornelius the centurion.

Under every dispensation of the Covenant of Redemption—Patriarchal, Abrahamic, Mosaic, or Christian—the children of Church members have ever been regarded as entitled to the signs and seals of the Covenant under which the Church existed as a Visible Institute. Noah's children were saved from the Flood with their righteous father and because of his faith; Abraham's children were included in the Covenant made with him, and received the sign of that Covenant, the circumcision of the flesh; the King Himself, when He was upon the earth, received the children, and declared that they were members of His heavenly kingdom; inspired Apostles recognized the birth-rights of the children of Church members, and baptized whole households of them; and the whole Christian Church, with few exceptions, has followed these illustrious examples.

CHAPTER XII.

The Lord's Supper, and the Law of Life.

GREAT events in the history of individuals and nations are commemorated by various kinds of ceremonies and observances.

Signal victories achieved by the Roman Emperors were commemorated by the erection of triumphal arches and columns. Remarkable events in the history of the Jews were commemorated by national feasts. The Independence of the United States of America is commemorated from year to year by the observance of the Fourth day of July as a great National Festival.

The column of Trajan at Rome is sufficient evidence to establish the fact that Trajan lived, that he was Emperor of Rome, and that he conquered the Dacians and Parthians. The observance of the Feast of Passover by the Jews is sufficient evidence to establish the facts connected with its institution more than three thousand years ago in Egypt. The unfinished monument of Washington at the Capital of the United States of America, and the observance of the anniversary of his birth by the American people, establish the fact that such a man as Washington lived; that he was born on the 22d day of February; and that he was the Father of his country.

In proportion too, as the commemorative observances are widespread and ever recurring, just in that proportion is the evidence increased that the events commemorated did actually occur. If no such event as the Independence of the United States has ever occurred, the observance of the Fourth day of July as the anniversary of that Independence by the whole American people would be simply impossible.

Now the great event in the history of the God-man and of His kingdom is commemorated by an observance called the Lord's Supper. The amount and character of the historic evidence accumulated upon this point leave no room whatever to doubt that since the death of Jesus Christ those who acknowledge Him as Lord and King have observed this ordinance in memory of His death. The observance of the Lord's Supper can be traced back as a historical fact to the night when Jesus Himself instituted the Supper.

What adds significance to this Memorial Feast as an evidence that such a man as Jesus did live and die is the fact, that the observance of this rite has not been confined to one age, or country, or people, or nation : it has been observed for eighteen centuries in all lands, among almost all people and nations. If Jesus did not institute this ordinance, and if it is not a memorial of His death, then its observance as above stated is no less remarkable than the greatest miracle recorded in the Bible ; nay, it is more marvelous than any miracle.

The Lord's Supper was instituted by Jesus Christ Himself, and before His death. Jesus and the Twelve went into the city of Jerusalem to eat the Passover Supper, one of the great national Feasts of the Jews; and while they were partaking of the meal, Jesus took bread, and blessed it, and brake it, and gave to His disciples, and said, Take, eat; this is my body which is given for you ; this do in remembrance of Me. And He took the cup, and gave thanks, and gave it to them, saying, Drink ye all of it ; for this is my blood of the New Testament which is shed for many for the remission of sins. And as often as Christians eat this bread and drink this cup, they do show the Lord's death till He comes.

The remarkable feature about this observance

is that it is a Memorial of the death of the Founder of the Christian Church. Nations and organizations among men never celebrate the death-days of their founders and heroes; they always select some joyous day or some triumphant event in the history of the man or the nation. Americans do not observe the anniversary of the death of Washington, but the anniversary of his birth; nor do they observe the anniversary of any of their defeats during Revolution, but the Fourth of July, the Independence anniversary, is observed. So with all other nations and organizations; the joyous and triumphant days are the anniversary days. Christ commanded His death to be commemorated because that event was the great significant event in His life; for this very end did He come into the world, that He might die. He was born to die. Strike the death of Christ from the Christian Calendar, and nothing is left; for the whole structure of the Christian Church rests upon Christ crucified as the *Chief Corner-stone*. The widespread observance of this Sacrament for so many centuries does incontestably establish the fact of the *death* of Jesus Christ; and this fact is the great central idea of the Christian Religion.

Another striking fact connected with this Supper is, that out of the most perishable elements of bread and wine an imperishable and perpetual memorial is erected. No brass, no bronze, no marble commemorates a Saviour's death; but the outward memorial of that event has survived the ravages of eighteen centuries; and all the experience of the past proves that it will remain the monument of that death, until He shall come a second time, without sin unto salvation.

The profound wisdom of Jesus, in appointing these perishable elements the perpetual memorial of His death, is abundantly evident, when we reflect upon the universal and invariable tendency of mankind, to attach an undue and superstitious importance to all sacred signs and relics.

The human mind, with all the light of Revelation, has ever sought to deify and worship the creature; and where the outward sign of a religious ordinance signified the very body and blood of the Incarnate God, how surely will fallen man be led to deify the sign, and worship the creature instead of the Creator! Christ ordains that the sign, though perpetual, shall consist of *perishable* elements. And men are under the necessity of creating a new Christ every time they deify, and worship the Consecrated Host.

When Jesus brake the bread, and gave to His

disciples, saying, This is my body broken for you, He does not mean to teach, that that very bread broken was His very body broken; nor that the very wine poured out was His very blood poured out; for His body had not as yet been broken, nor had His blood been shed; for He was crucified, and gave His body, and shed His blood, *after* He had instituted the Supper. What He does teach is, that the bread broken *signifies* His body broken, and the wine poured out signifies His blood poured. As in the Sacrament of Baptism, the water is not the Holy Ghost, but symbolizes the Holy Ghost, so here the bread is not Christ's body, but symbolizes that body, and the wine symbolizes His blood. One of the essential elements of a Sacrament is the *outward sign;* but if the bread be the real body, and the wine the real blood, then there is no outward sign, and hence no Sacrament: and the Holy Supper is but a cannibal feast of Christians, where they devour their Redeemer and drink His blood. God has revealed truths *above reason;* He has never revealed truth *contradictory of the senses*, and all the senses of all who have ever lived have been unable to detect real body or real blood in the Eucharist; there is bread and there is wine, but there is no body and no blood.

The outward sign, then, is undoubtedly the

bread and the wine. But a sign must signify something; and the thing signified by the bread and wine is the broken body and the shed blood of the Lord Jesus Christ. The Lord's Supper is the proclamation, by sensible signs, of Christ crucified. It is a pictorial representation of the sum and substance of the Gospel—Christ crucified, the Wisdom of God and the Power of God unto salvation; and to the believer it not only signifies Christ crucified, but *seals* to him all the benefits of that death.

There are two unalterable pre-requisites to man's being happy in the world to come. His sins must be pardoned, and his nature must be purified. He must have a title to heaven, and a fitness for heaven. These two ideas underlie the whole of Christ's work; and without the title to, and the fitness for, no man can enter the kingdom of heaven. Before the Incarnation of the Son of God, the Old Testament Church had the Sacrament of circumcision, wherein was signified the purification of man's nature, by the work of the Holy Ghost, and the Sacrament of the Passover, wherein was signified the pardon of the sinner, through the blood of the Lamb, that taketh away the sin of the world.

After the Incarnation, and in the New Testament Church, baptism takes the place of circumcision, and holds forth the Regeneration of the soul by the work of the Spirit; and the Lord's Supper takes the place of the Passover Supper, and holds forth the idea of pardon through the broken body and shed blood of Jesus Christ. As there can be but one New Birth of the soul, so Baptism, which is the sign therof, ought never be administered but once to the same person; but as the renewed soul sins often, and needs to be pardoned often, so the Lord's Supper, which is the sign thereof, is to be administered often to the same person. Baptism has reference to the *beginning* of the New Spiritual Life; the Lord's Supper to the *continued nourishment* of that Life. The New Life can have but *one* beginning; but it needs *continued* supplies of spiritual food.

Christ and all the blessings of the Covenant of Redemption are signed and sealed to the worthy recipient of the Sacrament of the Lord's Supper. To the believer in Jesus, the Lord's Supper not only signifies, it also *seals*, the blessings secured by Christ's death. Not that there is any inherent efficacy in the bread and wine, or that the Sacrament of itself confers grace; but the King in Zion has appended the sensible sign to His written and covenanted promises as the seal thereof. The seal, attached to the word of the King, does not make the

King's promise and word any more sure, but it wonderfully helps and strengthens the faith of the subject in the word of His Sovereign, wherein he is promised pardon and life eternal. And just as bread and wine nourish the natural life of the body, so this ordinance of the King does to the worthy communicant nourish the supernatural life of the soul. By *faith* he spiritually receives and feeds upon that spiritual food signified by the bread and wine.

The invisible grace in the soul of the subject of this Spiritual kingdom, answerable to the Sacrament of the Lord's Supper, is faith or allegiance to King Jesus.

The Christian's faith is no mere assent of the intellect to the truth of the teachings of the Divine man, nor any mere natural enthusiasm or goodness of the soul attaching itself to Jesus and His kingdom; it is not natural, but supernatural; it is the gift of God; it is a manifestation of the New Life communicated to the soul by the Holy Spirit; it is the very life of the Christian, for the just shall live by his faith. The renewed soul, looking through the Sacrament to Christ crucified, recognizes Him as Lord and King and Saviour, and as such it receives and rests upon Him as the only hope and foundation of salvation.

Faith is an act of the regenerated soul, but

not a mere act; it is rather a life; it is the continued resting of the soul upon the righteousness of the crucified Redeemer. The Lord's Supper brings the object of his faith specially near to the believer. This do in remembrance of Me. As the devout Christian receives the sacred emblems, he also receives, at the same time, spiritually, Him whom the emblems symbolize.

The Supper stands in the kingly authority of Christ, and is to be observed by the members of His kingdom because He commands it. This do in remembrance of Me, said the King; how dare His subjects disobey His direct and positive command?

The Lord's Supper is called a Sacrament; from the Latin *sacramentum*, an oath—the word denoting the oath of allegiance which the Roman soldier took to his emperor or general. So with the Christian soldier, the Supper is his *Sacramentum*, his oath of Allegiance to the Great Captain of his salvation: in this solemn act, he avows himself to be a loyal and faithful subject of King Jesus, and consecrates his life to the service of his rightful Lord.

The great law of life in the Spiritual kingdom of the God-man is the profound allegiance of every true subject to Him who is Head over the Church and King in Zion. This allegiance to the King is the overpowering passion of the New Creature in Christ Jesus; his devotion to the Great Captain is complete and absorbing, and his zeal for the prosperity of the kingdom is as a consuming fire in his bones: the love of Christ constrains him, and the zeal of Christ's House consumes him.

As the Christian soldier sits with the Great Captain at the Lord's table, and receives the Sacred memorials, his soul glows with the fire of a complete consecration, and as he communes, in a method unknown to the world, with his adorable Lord and Master, he renews his sacramentum, his oath of fidelity and allegiance to his King, and receives new measures of strength and grace for the Christian warfare. Talk not to this man of intellectual exercises, of natural admiration for the loveliness of the character of the man Jesus; with him, there is a Soul Union to the Deus-Homo; by faith he is feeding with and upon the Son of God, and this life of Faith is hid with Christ in God.

But the Lord's Supper is not only a sacramentum; it is also a Κοινονία, a Fellowship, a Communion. They who have the Life of Faith in their souls are not only one with Christ, and have fellowship with Him, but they are also one with each other, and have fellowship one with the other.

The Lord's Supper is the Communion meal of the saints, where the Unity of the Christian Church is visibly realized—where the members of the Spiritual kingdom, the subjects of King Jesus, having taken the vow of consecration to their common Lord, unite in partaking of a simple meal in token of their brotherhood. This communion of the Saints flows from their union and communion with their common Head and Saviour. The life of the God-man flows from Him through all the members who compose His mystical body; the Life of the Brotherhood is one, because it comes down from one glorious source, even the Risen Christ. That the unbelieving world, outside of this consecrated Brotherhood, should not comprehend these sacred and holy mysteries of the Spiritual kingdom is not at all to be wondered at. Men outside of the Masonic Order cannot understand the symbols of Masonry; they must be initiated and instructed in the principles of the Order. So a man must have the Spiritual Baptism and enter the Spiritual kingdom before he can understand the holy mysteries of that kingdom; the natural man receiveth not the things of the Spirit, neither can he understand them, for they are spiritually discerned. The things of God knoweth no man, but the Spirit of

God, and he to whom the Spirit shall reveal them. A man must do the will of God, before he can understand the doctrine. Even the things of a man must be discerned by the spirit of man; much more must there be a Spiritual discernment to understand the things of God.

This Supper is then a *separating* ordinance; it draws the line between those who acknowledge Jesus as their King, and those who will not have Him to rule over and reign in them. They who are loyal subjects of the crucified but risen King will joyfully obey His command—this *do* in remembrance of Me: loving Him, they will keep this command.

On the other hand, they who have never acknowledged this King as their King, this Saviour as their Saviour, will feel no obligation to obey a King whom they never acknowledged, and to vow allegiance to a Lord whom they do not love. And it is a fearful perjury for a man who does not love Jesus to come to the Lord's table, and take the *Sacramentum* and partake of the Holy Communion. He is vowing a lie in the presence of the Crucified but Omniscient Christ.

The simple test of admission to the Supper

is loyalty and love to Him whose table it is, and whose death it commemorates. If any man truly and sincerely loves Jesus, it is his privilege and duty to testify that love by partaking of the Supper.

CHAPTER XIII.

The Second Coming of the Son of Man.

UPON no topic is the unity of the faith of the Church of God more plainly seen, than in reference to the Second Coming of the Son of Man. Since the Resurrection, no part of the Visible Church has even a doubt as to the fact, that the Lord Jesus would come again. While the Church has been a unit in believing the fact of the Second Advent, there have been great diversities of views as to the time of, and the circumstances attending, that Advent. The Church could not doubt when the King Himself plainly said that He would come again and receive His people to Himself.

It will assist our inquiry in this discussion to divide the life of the Deus-Homo into the following periods:—

I. Period before the Incarnation;

II. Period after the Incarnation.

This division is not artificial, but perfectly natural; for it is evident that the assumption of human nature into personal union with the Divine nature does mark an era in the life of the Son of God.

The life of the Son of God before the Incarnation also falls into two natural divisions, viz :—

1. The eternal life of the Son before the creation of the material heavens and earth;

2. His Life from the Creation to the Incarnation.

Concerning His life before the Creation, we only know that He was in the beginning, and was with God, and was God.

From the Creation to the Incarnation, is a a period of about four thousand years; in which, He was revealing Himself to the race, and preparing the world for His coming in the flesh.

His Life, after the Incarnation is also capable of a natural division into two parts, viz :—

1. The time before the General Judgment;

2. The time after the General Judgment.

The first division here, from His Incarnation to the Judgment, is a period of Revelation, in which Christ is revealing Himself by His Spirit, Word, and Providence to His Church.

The second division of this period, like the first division of the first period, lies in comparative darkness. We know that all enemies are subdued under the Son; that He delivers up the kingdom to the Father, and that God is all in all. The beginning and the end of the life of the Son of God lie in the depths of the Infinities and Eternities, beyond the reach of mortal sight, save that we know that He always was and always will be; that part of His life that is let down from heaven into the history of men we do know; and we can also understand its grand facts, and their import.

The first division of the Second Period, viz.: from the Incarnation to the Judgment, may be thus subdivided:—

(*a.*) From His Incarnation to His Resurrection.

(*b.*) From His Resurrection to His Ascension.

(*c.*) From His Ascension to His Second Advent.

(*d.*) From the Second Advent to the General Judgment.

The first subdivision includes the childhood, youth, personal ministry and death of Jesus, covering a period of about thirty-three years and a half.

The second subdivision covers a period of about forty days, in which Jesus gave to chosen witnesses infallible proofs of His Resurrection.

The third subdivision is absolutely indefinite,

for no man knoweth the day or the hour of the coming of the Son of man.

The fourth subdivision extends over the mystic thousand years of the Revelation.

According to this chronology, the Advent closes the *third* subdivision of the *first* division of the *second* period.

There are points of resemblance and of contrast between the *first* coming of the Son of God in the flesh, and the *second* coming of the Son of man in glorified flesh.

At His first coming, He bare the sins of His people; at His second coming, He brings salvation to them: in the first, He who knew no sin was made sin for them; in the second, He comes without sin unto salvation.

There are two Testaments—the Old and the New; there are two comings of the Son of God—one in the flesh, the other in glory; His Incarnation was the great promise of the Old Testament; His second Advent is the great promise of the New.

The main object of all Old Testament Revelation was to prepare the race for the coming of the Promised Seed—that Seed of the woman, promised in Eden, to the lost parents of the race. As the covenant of Redemption is historically developed, additional light is thrown upon the Eden promise. The coming One shall descend from Shem, and unto Shiloh shall be the gathering of the people.

Out of the loins of Abraham shall He come, and in Him shall all the nations of the earth be blessed. As we approach nearer and nearer the time of His Advent, prophecy becomes clearer and clearer, until it would seem that when Jesus Christ was born in Bethlehem of Judea, no flesh could for a moment doubt that this was indeed the Seed promised in Eden, the Messiah of Old Testament Revelation, the Saviour of the world. And yet when He came unto His own, though they had in their hands all these clear prophecies concerning Him, they received Him not, but cried aloud for His blood, even when the pagan Pilate desired to release Him.

Now His second coming bears the same relation to the New, that His first coming bears to the Old Testament. As the Old Testament-Church looked forward, with hope and joy to the coming of Messiah, so the New Testament-Church, as she now waits weeping in the wilderness, looks forward with patience and expectation and longing for the hour when the Kingly Bridegroom shall return to wipe the tears from the face of His beloved Bride. As the whole of the Old Testament Revelation pointed forward to the coming Messiah, so the doctrine of the second Advent of the Son of Man is thoroughly inwoven into the entire fabric of New Testament Revelation. Many of those wondrous parables uttered by the Divine Man find their full solution only at His coming. The nobleman who took his journey into a far country; the servants to whom the Lord entrusted talents, until He should come and reckon with them; the five wise and the five foolish virgins, who are aroused at midnight by the coming of the Bridegroom,—these and others of His parables plainly teach the fact that He will come again.

The solemn Sacrament of the Lord's Supper, not only shows forth the death of the Divine man, but as often as it is administered, it shows forth that death, till He comes again.

The great historic questions of this Dispensation are to find their solution at and in the second coming of the Son of man. The Man of Sin who is now revealed, that son of perdition, who opposeth and exalteth himself above all that is called God or that is worshiped, will continue his career of wickedness, until the coming Lord shall consume him with the spirit of His mouth, and shall destroy him in Epiphany of His personality.

The relations of the Jews, God's ancient people, to the Covenant; the question of their ingrafting and restoration; their return to Judea, and the rebuilding of Jerusalem,—all of these questions are to receive a solution, one way or the other, at His appearing and His kingdom, when the veil shall be taken away from their hearts.

The great problem of the Pagan world, how far the Gospel is to be preached, and how many of the Gentiles are to be converted in the latter days, these and kindred problems will not be solved until He shall come.

Nay; so completely is this doctrine incorporated into the New Testament, that the exhortation to daily Christian duty is based upon the fact, that as we know not the hour of His coming, we ought to watch, pray, and be ready.

As Jesus knew and foretold His death, so He also knew and foretold that He would come again. He declared that if any one was ashamed of Him and His words, of him would He be ashamed, when He came in the glory of the Father with the holy angels. He said that all the tribes of the earth would mourn when the sign of the Son of man appeared in heaven, and that then the Son of man would be seen coming in the clouds of heaven, with power and great glory.

The declaration was also expressly made by angelic messengers to the Apostles, who were steadfastly gazing into heaven, whither Jesus had gone, Ye men of Galilee, why stand ye gazing up into heaven? This same Jesus which is taken up from you into heaven shall so come *in like manner* as ye have seen Him go into heaven. This statement is so clear and explicit that it is impossible for it to mean anything else than the personal return of the Godman in His glorified human body.

After His resurrection, Jesus was seen of His followers for about forty days, and then, as they were assembled at the mountain in Galilee where Jesus had appointed to meet them, He was parted from them and ascended up into heaven, where He will remain until the times of the Restitution of all things.

After His obedience and sacrifice, God exalted Him, raising from the dead, and giving Him a name that is above every name, that at the name of Jesus every knee should bow and every tongue should confess.

The Mediator of the Covenant having performed all of its stipulations, ascended up on high, leading captivity captive, and giving gifts unto men: as His humiliation was infinite, so also His exaltation is infinite; for He is made Head over all things. He went up to heaven with a shout, and the pearly gates lifted up their heads, and the everlasting doors were lifted up, and the crowned King entered in and took possession of His Mediatorial throne; and was welcomed back to His heavenly home by the shining ranks of angels and archangels, cherubim and seraphim, principalities and powers. When He comes again, He will descend from heaven, not as the wayfaring man turning aside to tarry for the night, but as mighty King, with a shout and the voice of the archangel and the trump of God.

He will come in like manner as He was taken up. Then He was escorted by a great cloud of angels: when He returns the same heavenly messengers will attend Him, for He will come in the glory of the Father with the holy angels.

He came once in the form of a servant and after the fashion of a man; His face was so marred, and His form more than the sons of men; the chastisement of our peace was upon Him, and by His stripes we were healed. His hands were pierced by the nails, and His side with the soldier's spear. This same Jesus, this crucified but Risen Christ, in His glorified human body will surely come again. But not then will He come as the Man of sorrows and acquainted with grief, hiding as it were His face from us; not then as the Lamb of God, slain from the foundation of the world; not then as the world's atoning Sacrifice; but as the world's avenging Judge, as the Lion of the tribe of Judah, as the mighty King in Zion, and as Judge of the quick and dead.

He will come in all the pomp of His power and in all the splendor of the skies; His eyes as a flame of fire, and His feet like unto fine brass, as if they burned in a furnace; the crown of many diadems upon His head, and the seven stars in His right hand. He is attended by thousands and tens of thousands of holy angels; the majestic train sweeps down in solemn grandeur from the skies; the voice of the archangel and the pealing notes of the trump of of God are heard, and lo! the Crucified has returned in triumph to the earth.

At His first coming, when He came unto His own, they received Him not, for the Jewish Church was hopelessly apostate; and He himself asks the thrilling question, Nevertheless, when the Son of man cometh, shall He find faith on the earth?

There are many who declare that the whole earth will be filled with the knowledge of the Lord at the coming of the Son of man; that then the Gospel will have been proclaimed to all the nations of the earth; and that in a season of universal peace, righteousness, and love Jesus will return to the earth: and that, in reply to the Saviour's question, the true answer is, Yea, Lord, the whole earth will be full of faith.

There are three great eras in the history of the race, each marked by a peculiar form of religion, by a peculiar form of wickedness; and each one terminated by a signal display of the Divine power.

The first era extends from the Creation to the Deluge, a period of about sixteen hundred years; this era was marked by the outbreaking wickedness of the children of men; and during this era religion assumed the Family *form:* the Church and State both existed in the bosom of the family, neither one of them being fully organized or established among men. During this period family religion did not bring men to God; but on the contrary, at its close, the whole race had utterly and hopelessly departed from God; and in the midst of the abounding iniquity of the antediluvian world, the Lord descended in vengeance, and terminated the era and closed the career of the race by the waters of the Flood, that destroyed the whole family of man, save Noah and those with him in the Ark: as it was in the days of Noah, so shall also the coming of the Son of man be.

The second era extends from the Deluge to time of the first Advent, a period of about twenty-three hundred years. Although the Patriarchal form of religion prevailed during the first part of this period, still the era was characterized by a *national* form of religion: the worship of God was in the chosen Nation. The peculiar form of wickedness in this era was *idolatry*—leaving the worship and service of the true God for idols. But a national form of religion proved no more efficacious in drawing men to God than had the family, and when God was manifested in the flesh, all flesh was thoroughly corrupt. And the old economy passed away when the veil of the temple was rent, and the chosen nation was scattered to the four quarters of the earth when their Temple was destroyed. Neither at the flood, nor at His Incarnation, did the Son of man find faith when He came to the earth: will He find it when He comes again?

The third era extends from the destruction of the temple until the second Advent. In this period the prevailing form of religion is the Church, as a visible, separate, spiritual institute among men. The peculiar form of wickedness is neither violence nor idolatry, but *apostasy*—men departing from the truth, and holding the truth in unrighteousness: men of sin and sons of perdition sit now even in the temple of God, and in His name work their vilest iniquity. The apostasy of Mohammed in the East still flourishes in wondrous vigor, and almost one-tenth of the human race bow their faces to Mecca, and cry God is great, and Mohammed is His only prophet. The Harlot rides forth still upon her mystic Beast, and one-fourth of the population of the globe follow in her train; while the great mass of mankind lie in the cold and deadly embrace of heathenism, and evil men wax worse and worse. When the Bridegroom comes, *all ten* Virgins are asleep, and only *five* have any oil in their lamps.

This era is a pre-eminently a religious age, in name at least. Religious rites, forms, ceremonies, words, rituals, establishments abound; even the most infamous men open the most infamous partisan and political meetings with prayer to God: certainly the *form* of godliness is beautiful and robust, but alas! many who have the form deny the power thereof. The Divine Teacher does not give us any reason to suppose that this state of things will be better until He comes again; when He comes, He does not expect to find much real saving faith in the earth.

When He returns it will not be to find the Church and the world holy and righteous and ready to receive Him, but to find an apostate Church and a guilty and corrupt world. He will come in flaming fire to execute judgment, and that judgment must begin first at the house of God. The harvest of the earth will then be ripe for the reaping, and the angels will separate the wheat from the tares, and bind the tares in bundles for the everlasting burning.

He will raise His righteous dead, transfigure His righteous living, destroy the wicked from the earth, purify the earth with fire, and make the new heavens and the new earth for the dwelling of the righteous.

The order of the Resurrection is—Christ the first-fruits; then they that are Christ's at His coming. Only the righteous have part in the first Resurrection, which occurs at His Advent: the rest of the dead live not until the thousand years are ended. This is the Resurrection for which Paul hopes, when he says, If by any means I might attain unto the Resurrection *from among* the dead. This is the Resurrection of the Just, of which Jesus speaks. This is the *first* resurrection, spoken of in the Revelation.

When the Lord descends from heaven, the righteous are caught up with Him in the air, while the new heavens and the new earth are being prepared for the saints. After the fire purification of earth, the saints descend to possess the renovated earth.

The wicked who are alive at His coming are

punished with everlasting destruction from the presence of the Lord.

The righteous who are alive are transfigured, and caught up with the risen righteous.

His coming will establish His kingdom in power and great glory. The Church is now a *regnum crucis*—then it will be a *regnum gloriæ;* and Jésus will then be glorified *in* his saints, and admired *in* all them that believe.

Of the day and the hour of the coming of the Son of man knoweth no man, no, not even the angels in heaven, but the Father only. That day is wisely and purposely kept hid from all created eyes: it will come suddenly and unexpectedly, as a thief in the night. As it was in the days of Noah, so shall also the coming of the Son of man be: they were eating and drinking, marrying and giving in marriage, and knew *not until* the Flood came and took them all away; so also will it be when He appears— the day will not be known *until* the day comes. As a snare will it come on all them that dwell on the face of the whole earth. When the Lord Himself so plainly teaches that the day is not, and cannot be known until it comes, it is very strange that men should undertake to determine definitely the day of His appearing and His kingdom. As it is absolutely impossible to fix certainly the *terminus a quo* of the prophetic periods that determine the time of His coming, of course it is impossible to settle the *terminus ad quem*.

It is true that there are certain signs that precede the great and notable day of the Lord; and they who study most devoutly the prophetic signs will be able to form a more accurate judgment of the times and seasons than those who neglect the prophecies.

The signs that precede His coming are great apostasies, false Christs, false prophets, wars and rumors of war, perilous times, abounding iniquities, great political commotions, evil men waxing worse and worse, the seas and waves roaring, and men's hearts failing them for fear, and looking for the things that are coming on the earth; earthquakes, famines, and pestilences; signs in the sun and moon, and stars; on earth distress of nations and perplexities,—when these things begin to come to pass, then let the saints lift up their heads and look, for their Redemption draweth nigh.

Heaven and earth shall pass away, but His words shall never pass until all is fulfilled. He that testifieth these things saith, Surely I come quickly. Amen. Even so come, Lord Jesus.

THE END.

www.ingramcontent.com/pod-product-compliance
Lightning Source LLC
Chambersburg PA
CBHW020908230426
43666CB00008B/1366